1
1

unlimited

TREASURY
OF
SUCCESS
UNLIMITED

edited by
OG MANDINO

A Publication of
The Napoleon Hill Foundation

Published by:
    The Napoleon Hill Foundation
    P. O. Box 1277
    Wise, Virginia 24293

    Website: www.naphill.org
    Email: napoleonhill@uvawise.edu

Distributed by:
    Executive Books
    206 W. Allen Street
    Mechanicsburg, PA 17055

    Telephone: 800-233-2665
    Website: www.executivebooks.com

ISBN: 978-1-933715-62-9

PREFACE

Success is one of the most difficult words in the English language to define. To you it may mean fame and personal power, to another it may be the acquisition of a million dollars, to many it is a happy home filled to capacity with love. Whatever your own personal definition of success may be, you will discover much to ponder in the pages of this book.

Since its first issue in 1954, *Success Unlimited* magazine has been guided by the philosophy, principles and personal efforts of one man—Editor and Publisher W. Clement Stone—and few living Americans write or speak on this subject of success with more authority or experience. His own success story transcends, by far, the heroes of the Horatio Alger stories he read as a young man. Beginning as a newsboy on the streets of Chicago, Mr. Stone applied many of the principles you will find in this book to amass, and share with others, a fortune that is in excess of $160 million!

With such a man at its helm, it is inevitable that *Success Unlimited* attracts to its pages nearly every giant in the field of self-help and inspirational writing. The best of their articles which have appeared in the magazine have been chosen for its first *Treasury of Success Unlimited.* You are about to meet people like Norman Vincent Peale, Napoleon Hill, Harold Sherman, Preston Bradley, Ben Sweetland and dozens of others who will show you how to become a whole person—not just wealthy, but also healthy, happy and wise.

Oliver Wendell Holmes once said that many ideas grow better when they are transplanted to another mind. You are about to discover a treasure chest of success ideas. Just one of them could change your entire life! May the ones you transplant from the following pages *to you* grow strong and healthy within your mind and heart until you blossom into the person you've always wanted to become.

OG MANDINO
Executive Director, *Success Unlimited*

CONTENTS

INTRODUCTION

by W. CLEMENT STONE

Editor and Publisher, *Success Unlimited*

Think and Grow Rich by Napoleon Hill was first published in 1937. Millions read it. I did too. It played an important part in motivating me and many thousands who were seeking happiness, health, power and wealth to achieve our objectives.

But there were hundreds of thousands of readers who found *Think and Grow Rich* so extremely interesting to read that they were carried away by the stories it contained and therefore did not recognize, study and use the principles that were applicable to themselves. Yes, they were momentarily inspired and undoubtedly benefited to some degree. But after reading the book, they failed to experience the success in life they had the capacity to achieve.

In 1952 I met Napoleon Hill for the first time. Because I had seen the power of *Think and Grow Rich* change the lives of thousands of persons for the better, I encouraged him to come out of retirement and spend five years to complete his life's work. He agreed on one condition . . . that I become his general manager. I accepted because I realized that it is seldom that one man can affect the lives of the masses of future generations.

It is no longer true that if you build the best mousetrap, a path will be beaten to your door. Today the best ideas, services and products must be sold. By vocation I was a salesman and sales manager. I felt that I had a contribution to make in marketing what we subsequently called the PMA (Positive Mental Attitude) concepts.

Principles: Use Them or You Lose Them

During the ten years Napoleon Hill and I were associated, our lectures, books, movies, personal consultations and the magazine *Success Unlimited* developed gratifying, effective, and often amazing results. Through them we inspired and taught individuals how to motivate themselves and others, at will, to acquire the true riches of life as well as monetary wealth and business success. We soon observed, however, that many individuals forgot the principles. They did not learn and employ them well enough to develop them as habits of thought. They lost their inspiration . . . they stopped trying.

We realized that motivation (inspiration to action) is like a fire: the flames will be extinguished unless the fire is refueled. In 1954 vitamins were the rage. We conceived the idea of the monthly magazine *Success Unlimited* to supply regular mental vitamins to revitalize those who were seeking self-help and wished inspiration to keep the flames of their enthusiasm for self-development alive.

So in 1954 Napoleon Hill and I founded *Success Unlimited*. Because of the many requests for an anthology, this book, *A Treasury of Success Unlimited*, was compiled.

Follow a Successful Guide

A Treasury of Success Unlimited can guide you to happiness, good physical and mental health, power and wealth. Like the book *Think and Grow Rich*, each biography, editorial or story is interesting reading. Each contains a message especially for you. Each is designed to stimulate you to develop the unlimited power of your mind.

The many successful authors who themselves use the principles of success revealed in their articles, and who, collectively, have influenced the lives of millions of persons for the better, give you guidelines which you can use to acquire happiness, good health and wealth, and eliminate unnecessary illness and misery.

We do not claim that the anthology in itself will bring happiness, health, power and wealth. But we do know that if you are seeking these, you will generate new ideas and be persistently motivated toward your objectives as you read each chapter. Your life will be changed, for you will be motivated to read inspirational, self-help books which are referred to—books which have already changed countless thousands of lives for the better. You will like the concepts of certain authors and will wish to read their works. In brief, you will recognize new opportunities that were not previously apparent to you. But most of all, when you have a good idea, you will be impelled to follow through with . . . action.

Are You Ready?

Improved good health and happiness can be yours. Wealth . . . you can get it. Power . . . you have it within you. But you must decide whether you are willing to pay the price to extract and use the success principles necessary to acquire these riches to life. The choice is yours and . . . yours alone.

Perhaps you are ready to discover and use gems of thought—simple universal principles—contained in *A Treasury of Success Unlimited.* Perhaps you are not. If you are not ready, but wish to increase your happiness, physical and mental health, power and wealth, you can prepare yourself *now* by determining specifically what you really want to achieve or acquire. For when you know what your specific objectives are concerning your distant, intermediate and immediate goals, you will be more apt to recognize that which will help you achieve them.

If you have a sincere desire to achieve anything worthwhile in life, an affirmation answer to the following questions will indicate that you are ready to get for yourself the most this book has to offer. Are you willing to pay the price:

> To try to be honest with yourself and recognize your strengths and weaknesses?
>
> To try to engage in self-inspection with regularity?
>
> To try to discover how to develop desirable habits and eliminate those you are convinced are undesirable?
>
> To try to follow the rules revealed to you in this book which you yourself believe will help you to reach your distant, intermediate and immediate goals?
>
> To try to recognize the principles that are applicable to you?

If you are not willing to pay the price . . . if you are not ready

. . . then enjoy the book. You'll like it. In all probability your reaction will be such that you will then be ready to reread it and extract the principles that can help you bring your wishes into reality. For each chapter will be thought-provoking as each author endeavors to motivate you to desirable action.

Results Are What Count

In 1952 I made a resolution. I resolved that I would not write an article, write a book or give a speech unless I endeavored to motivate the reader or member of my listening audience to desirable action. I haven't failed to live up to that resolution. This introductory to *A Treasury of Success Unlimited* is no exception. For I am attempting to motivate you to seek and find greater happiness, good mental and physical health, power and wealth, by suggesting you endeavor to recognize, relate, assimilate and use the principles contained in each chapter of this book.

I evaluate my work by the standard: Results are what count. I feel warranted in speaking with authority. The type of material used in this anthology has been instrumental in building Combined Insurance Company of America, of which I am president, into the largest company of its kind in the world. Every sales representative, office employee and shareholder in the Combined Group of Companies (which includes the Combined Insurance Company of America, Combined American Insurance Company, Hearthstone Insurance Company of Massachusetts and First National Casualty Company) has received such information for many years. I have firsthand knowledge of its effectiveness.

Also, as president of the Chicago Boys Club, I have seen the lives of teenage boys who have been exposed to such inspirational literature changed for the better.

Recidivism has been reduced in prisons where inspirational self-help books and *Success Unlimited* magazine have been furnished to those who were incarcerated, and where they were instructed in the principles contained in this literature.

Letters from many subscribers in the United States and other parts of the world, whom I have not met, indicate the help and inspiration they have received from the magazine.

Therefore, from firsthand experience and testimonials I

know that *Success Unlimited* has been a powerful influence in bringing happiness, health, power and wealth to those who had a sincere desire to achieve their specific objectives.

The selected articles from *Success Unlimited* issues of the past, contained in *A Treasury of Success Unlimited,* can do for you what the magazine has done for others.

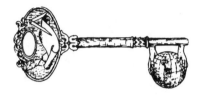

1

YOU UNLIMITED

Of all knowledge the wise and good
seek most to know themselves.
—Shakespeare

Do you believe you have unlimited possibilities
for happiness and success?
You will, after you read. . .

YOU UNLIMITED

by DR. PRESTON BRADLEY

Many years ago I was walking across the old Rush Street Bridge in Chicago with my coat-collar up and a cap pulled down over my eyes, and I bumped into a man who had on a heavy raincoat and was walking in the opposite direction, with his head down and his hat pulled over his eyes. I said, "I'm sorry, excuse me." He said, "That's quite all right: I want to know if you like the rain, too." I looked into his face and knew immediately, for it was not many evenings before that I had sat in a theater and had seen him in an interpretation of one of the great classic plays of our literature—the play of Peer Gynt—for the man to whom I was speaking, who became my friend until his death, was that fine, distinguished gentleman, scholar and great actor, Richard Mansfield, who had to struggle and fight to read that enviable position which he occupied in the American Theater as one of the great interpreters of the classics.

Mr. Mansfield never remembered when he did not want to become a great actor. As a child, like a great many children, he loved to mimic people. His mother opposed him in his ambition very bitterly. She wanted him to go into business and follow the mercantile profession. This was revolting to Mansfield, and he played his first part when he was a lad of seventeen. His mother thought she would humiliate and embarrass him sufficiently so that he never would think of the theater again. At the opening performance of the play, in which he had a very minor part, she and two of her friends engaged seats not far from the front of the stage. When this boy, with his dreams of greatness in the theater—and at its best it is a noble profession, with great social and cultural values—came on in the play, he was publicly ridiculed by his mother. She taunted him! She and her friends laughed, whispered and did everything in the world they could to defeat him. He went through his part, but he said he went to his dressing room and wept bitterly. It seemed that the world had dropped away from him that he should be treated like that, but he said to himself: "I will take my life and develop every bit of it to the perfection of my art. No one can stop me. I believe that I have unlimited possibilities and I will do my best to develop them." Nothing stopped him. Early in life he realized that he was not limited by any influence that could be constructed about him to defeat the highest purposes of his life.

Now, are we all constituted in such a way that our success in life consists of decreasing our limitations? Is it possible for us to have such a clear conception of what those limitations are that we can make it our supreme business to decrease them? Most of us are very poor critics of ourselves. We can easily criticize others and discover what is wrong with them, and we can easily build up an argument for our own side of the situation; but it is a far more difficult thing to be a self-critic—to take the situation that comes into our life and sit down with it frankly and say: "What did I do, or what have I said that has contributed to this situation?"

There is not a person reading this article who is living up to his or her own possibilities. If you feel in pretty much of a chaos, frustrated, lots of trouble and worry, just turn the searchlight on yourself and you will discover an available source of power. When you open up the channels and the avenues for that power, it will flood your soul and you will find yourself developing strength and poise, a solidarity, a feeling of security, that nothing on earth can shake!

Is there jealousy in your heart? Is there envy? Opposition? Don't expect a miracle if you retain an obstacle. There is some disciplining you must do. You have got to clear out the old festering sores of your heart. Perhaps you have lied about someone; perhaps you have been unkind; perhaps you have slandered and gossiped. Perhaps you have been "little" when you should have been "big."

How can we transmit our ideals into action so that these ideals can have sway in our lives? Well, we have to begin in our own hearts. When we clear away all that clutters up the channels, the heart and mind are cleansed, the head becomes rarified and the old jealousies, animosities and hatreds are uprooted, and then, though trouble may come in and flood and encompass our lives, there still is a power that reveals our own possibilities. The mere fact that none of us is living up to his best does not predicate that we never can.

Set no barriers for yourself. Admit no barricades or obstacles. Anything in the way? Look at it, examine it, analyze your own relationship to the self-construction of it, clean up your own life and there will be an influx of that power to which there is no limit—unlimited you! You are unlimited! There is no limit for you!

I knew a woman not many years ago who was stricken with polio—infantile paralysis—and as happens so frequently with adults, the resultant paralysis was tragic. One of those well-meaning ladies, you know the type, came into her sick-room where she was experiencing the tragedy of it, and said to her: "Oh, my dear, I suppose an illness like this *does* color one's life, doesn't it?" And this great soul replied, "Yes, it does color one's life, but I choose the color!"

The trouble is, in this complicated period in which we are all living, the very atmosphere is charged with frustration—and assault upon unity and harmony; discord is the theme. We are in chaos. And what is true of the world society is true of our little individual world, the one inside us that is so important to us. The world basically and fundamentally is constituted on the basis of harmony. Everything works in co-operation with something else. In the entire world of the physical universe every law is dovetailed into every other. The whole cosmic reality is integrated by one harmonic whole, and whenever discord anywhere comes into the picture, trouble arises. That is not only true of the cosmos of which we are a part, but it is also true of your life and mine in the little orbit in which we live.

How can we develop a technique for the manifestation of harmony, in spite of the storms around us? How can we keep our own integration in such operations so that disease and discord and confusion can never touch a single iota of our own constituency? Is that possible? Not entirely possible, though it was for some who have lived: Saint Francis of Assisi, the immortal and everlasting Gandhi, and I think for Dr. Albert Schweitzer down in the wilds and jungles of Africa, and for the classic example of all the history of humanity—the Master of Men. All the evil that can be designed against you can be dissipated and eradicated by the presence of that divine harmony. There is strength and beauty in it, nothing fragile or weak. It is strong; it is unlimited; for beauty is power; truth has vitality; unity has power. They are the great, positive, creative, unlimited forces of life. I like in this connection to think of some lines from a poem of Ella Wheeler Wilcox:

> You will be what you will be;
>   Let failure find its false content
> In that poor word "environment";
>   But spirit scorns it and is free.
> Be not impatient in delay,
>   But wait as one who understands;
> When spirit rises and commands
>   The gods are ready to obey.
>
> The river seeking for the sea
>   Confronts the dam and precipice,
> Yet knows it cannot fail or miss;
>   You will be what you will be!

Even without worldly wealth it's possible for you to . . .

BE GENEROUS!

by W. CLEMENT STONE

Be generous! Give to those whom you love; give to those who love you; give to the fortunate; give to the unfortunate; yes—give especially to those to whom you don't want to give.

Your most precious, valued possessions and your greatest powers are invisible and intangible. No one can take them. You, and you alone, can give them. You will receive abundance for your giving. The more you give—the more you will have!

Give a smile to everyone you meet (smile with your eyes)— and you'll smile and receive smiles. . .

Give a kind word (with a kindly thought behind the word)— you will be kind and receive kind words. . .

Give appreciation (warmth from the heart)—you will appreciate and be appreciated. . .

Give honor, credit and applause (the victor's wreath)—you will be honorable and receive credit and applause. . .

Give time for a worthy cause (with eagerness)—you will be worthy and richly rewarded. . .

Give hope (the magic ingredient for success)—you will have hope and be made hopeful. . .

Give happiness (a most treasured state of mind)—you will be happy and be made happy. . .

Give encouragement (the incentive to action)—you will have courage and be encouraged. . .

Give cheer (the verbal sunshine)—you'll be cheerful and cheered. . .

Give a pleasant response (the neutralizer of irritants)—you

will be pleasant and receive pleasant responses. . .

Give good thoughts (nature's character builder)—you will be good and the world will have good thoughts for you. . .

Give prayers (the instrument of miracles) for the godless and the godly—you will be reverent and receive blessings, more than you deserve!

Be generous! Give!

There are two things you can do when you make
a mistake. You can feel sorry for yourself
and give up or you can learn. . .

HOW TO PROFIT
FROM YOUR MISTAKES

by DOUGLAS LURTON

So you have made a mistake or many mistakes! So have we all.
But all do not realize that there are intelligent ways as well as
stupid ways of confronting errors. The smart approach is to
recognize that it's not so much the mistakes you have made as
what you do about those mistakes that really counts—on your
job, in a career, in dealing with others at home and elsewhere.
You can duck and dodge and alibi and mope and give up trying
to eliminate and correct mistakes, or you can use your head and
profit from your own errors and those of others.

1. You profit by facing mistakes squarely. Don't alibi.

Man's ego is such that he has an instinctive urge to alibi
failure and rationalize what he does, particularly when he makes
mistakes. That way he loses. He profits, however, if he intelligently faces up to mistakes, accepts responsibility, and doesn't
hide in a fog of his alibis. He profits when he refuses to become
a fugitive from the reality of his errors.

You probably recognize the other fellow's alibis more clearly
than your own. You know the folks who in a boom blame the
inflation, in a depression blame the season or the weather or the
dog or the cat.

Perhaps he who alibis and runs way from his problems may
live to alibi another day, but he's not likely to be a winner. You
can rationalize yourself into a rut of mediocrity or even into an
asylum. You can alibi yourself out of a job or out of a promotion.
There is a study of why thousands were fired from scores of

corporations.   More were discharged for sheer carelessness, more for simple failure to cooperate, more for plain unadulterated laziness, than for lack of specific skill on the job.   And yet it is safe to say that every one of these thousands of failures had a list of perfect alibis and refused to face up to his or her mistakes.

2. You profit if you don't let mistakes get you down.

The strong men and women bounce back after making mistakes.   They have the courage to try to avoid repetition of errors and to improve.   The weaklings make mistakes and don't bounce back.   They develop fear of trying again and having to make good.   They wallow in regrets for past errors.   Self-pity is a spoiler.   Remorse is a saboteur that can hold you back on any job and in any walk of life.

Babe Ruth whammed out home runs, but also fanned 1330 times and didn't sulk about it.   Thomas Edison made countless mistakes in his laboratories.   Abraham Lincoln failed in many ventures.   The notable inventor Charles F. Kettering would be the last to claim he never made a mistake.   But all of these countless others in more obscure places had one thing in common—they didn't let their mistakes get them down.   They recognized that courage has magic in it, and they bounced back after failure and tried again—and won.

3. You profit if you learn how to take criticism.

The first, almost instinctive reaction to criticism is resentment.   Your feelings are hurt! Your ego seems under attack, and an assault on your ego is like a small attack on your life.   Many of us resent even our own self-critical thoughts and dismiss them quickly.   The multitude resents criticism coming from others and sets up face-saving defenses.   But the smart, fully mature man or woman determines to profit from criticism and learns how to take it intelligently.

Adverse criticism may be offered from downright meanness or carelessness; or it may come from a sincere desire to help.   Anyone interested in self-advancement should listen to criticism either mean or honestly offered with this in mind: *The more true the criticism may be, the more it may hurt.*   Unjust criticism can be rather easily brushed to one side, but if it really stings, the intelligent approach is to seek out the elements of truth that may be involved and take steps to avoid any possible repetition of the criticism.

There is nothing fundamentally new here. It has all been said before and in fewer words by an ancient and wise king named Solomon: "Reprove not thy scorner, lest he hate thee; rebuke a wise man and he will love thee."

4. You profit most by learning from your own mistakes and those of others.

Learning from mistakes is a neat trick that you can acquire if you want to. It is a neat trick because actually we don't necessarily learn much by so-called experience. That may seem to be a challenging statement—and it is. But it is a statement that can be proved easily.

A doctor with fifty years of experience is not necessarily a better doctor than one with ten years of experience. A half-century as a craftsman does not necessarily mean that an individual is better than one with a few years of experience. It all depends on how alert the individual is, how selective he is in piling up his experience.

For instance, "experienced" bricklayers laid bricks for thousands of years in very much the same old way. From generation to generation master bricklayers repeated the methods they had been taught as apprentices. Their instruction included *experience in repeating the mistakes as well as the skills* of their craft. They learned to lay brick through experience, but they didn't learn from mistakes how to eliminate much lost motion, much of doing it the hard way. It was not until Dr. Frank Gilbreth studied the old "experienced" methods and applied a bit of scientific analysis that experienced bricklayers were taught how to lay many more bricks in much less time and with much less effort.

Unless we learn how to ferret our mistakes and learn from them, all too many of us may practice our mistakes as assiduously as we practice our successes.

John D. Rockefeller was a master at analyzing his mistakes as well as his successes. Each night Rockefeller set aside ten minutes during which he reviewed and analyzed what he had done during the day. He was critical of all of his actions and judgments and studied them carefully to sort out the mistakes when they occurred, to analyze them, to learn from them.

In his way Rockefeller was using the "scientific" approach to benefit from his mistakes. It is an approach that is used either consciously or unconsciously by all desiring to profit from mistakes and succeed in their occupational and home life and their relations with other people. Here are the steps:

Step one—Determine carefully just what it is you are trying to accomplish and why. What is the job of the moment? What is its purpose?

Step two—What are the pertinent facts involved? Can you get additional facts bearing on your problem from friends, from reading, from associates and leaders or others in a position to know?

Step three—After considering all of the facts available you should be able to determine various possible courses of action and consider each possible course carefully. Study both its advantages and its disadvantages.

Step four—Narrow down the possible courses of action to the one that comes closest to accomplishing your purpose.

Step five—If you have carefully followed the first four steps and not done a lot of conclusion-jumping, you may be sure that your analysis has given you the one best course of action for you, and the important step is to do something about it, beginning now.

5. You learn by taking courage from the fact that others, even the famous, make mistakes also.

There is a certain measure of comfort for all of us in knowing that there is no man or woman who hasn't made mistakes. No doubt it was this fact that prompted the humorist Mark Twain to point out that *man is the only animal who blushes—or needs to!*

There is rarely a biography or autobiography that doesn't reveal painful and sometimes costly mistakes. Many mistakes are hidden, but many are broadcast to the world. Not long ago an entire book was filled with the boners and bloopers of scores of the most noted radio and television stars—and when you stumble on the air millions know it!

There can and have been mistakes before the throne and in the seclusion of laboratory or home or factory. Sir Walter Scott, backing away from King George IV of England, sat down hard and smashed a goblet as well as his composure; but his blushes didn't hold him down. Mistakes in full or in part were responsible for certain wallboards, vulcanized rubber, Xrays, aniline colors, photography, dynamite, fiber glass, and many other inventions by people who learned from mistakes.

It is no crime to make mistakes as long as you are trying. It is, however, almost a crime against yourself, at least, to just be around and do nothing. And the gravest mistake of all is to continue practicing mistakes without learning to minimize or eliminate those errors.

It's not the mistakes you make, but what you do about those mistakes that really counts.

*Life will double in enjoyment for you
when you finally realize that. . .*

NOW IS YOUR TIME!

By DR. LOUIS BINSTOCK

No man can be said to be truly happy unless he has attained peace of mind—an inner security—a calm contentment. A man may experience many joys but he is not necessarily happy. He may know many pleasures but he is not necessarily happy. One of the best definitions of happiness that has crossed my reading road is one fashioned by William Henry Channing, Chaplain of the House of Representatives in the middle of the last century: "To live content with small means, to seek elegance rather than luxury and refinement rather than fashion; to be worthy not respectable, and wealthy not rich; to study hard, think quietly, talk gently, act frankly; to listen to the stars and birds, to babes and sages with open heart; to bear all cheerfully, do all bravely, await occasions, hurry never; in a word, to let the spiritual unbidden and unconscious grow up through the common."

The ancient rabbis have put it in this wise: "Who is rich? Only the man who rejoices in his portion, that is, the contented man." Perhaps no better solution has been found than the one discovered by Granpa Tubbs who had been stubborn and crabbed for years. No one in the village could please him. Then, overnight, he changed. Only sweetness and light radiated from his personality. The villagers were astounded. "Granpa," they cried, "what is it that caused you to change so suddenly?" "Well, sir," the old man replied, "I've been striving all my life for a contented mind. It's done no good. So I've just decided to be contented without it."

Some years ago I saw Joe E. Brown in the play *Harvey*. He

was the shining star of the production. Afterwards, I had the pleasure of meeting him. I asked him what he liked most about the play. He replied: "The line in which Harvey's drink-happy friend says, 'I always have a wonderful time just where I am, whoever I am with.'" I have thought about that line a great deal and the more I have thought about it, the more I have become convinced that Joe E. Brown was right. The basic lesson we must learn is that you cannot conquer reality by running away from it. You must meet and deal with it wherever it is, whenever it is, however it is, with whomever it is. There is the best place and really the only place where you can find lasting happiness.

Some time ago, while reading the biography of the Dutch painter Vincent Van Gogh, who struggled in poverty and pain all his days and died at too young an age, it would seem, to have reaped a sufficient reward for all his sacrifice and suffering, I ran across a significant passage in a letter to his brother Theo. It reads: "It would not make me so melancholy, Brother, if you had not added something that worries me. You say 'let's hope for better times.' You see, that is one of those things we must be careful of. To hope for better times must not be a feeling but an action in the present. For the very reason that I felt strongly the hope for better times, I threw myself with all my strength into the work of the present without thinking of the future." Van Gogh was not satisfied just to *hope* for better times. He toiled and sweated in order to *make* better times. He lived a short time but he left a glorious heritage to mankind.

Too many of us waste our years waiting for better times in the future or wondering about better times in the past, instead of working for better times in the present. If only we had lived in better times or had been born in better times! If only we lived with better people or belonged to a less underprivileged and despised group! If only we lived in a better home or a better town! If only we had a better business or a better job! If—if—if! Tomorrow—tomorrow—tomorrow! But today is always here; yesterday is gone, and tomorrow may never come. No, now is the time—here is the place. This is the person. This is your home. This is your job. This is your wife—your husband—your child—your mother—your friend. This is your people. This is your country. This is your generation. You can have a wonderful time just where you are, just when you are, just how you are, just with whomever you are.

2
FAITH UNLIMITED

All the scholastic scaffolding falls, as a ruined edifice, before one single word—faith.

—Napoleon

Death was minutes away when he discovered. . .

THE POWER OF PRAYER

by BILL NELSON

The tall handsome Irish tenor gasped for air. He was only vaguely aware of his bed in a Milwaukee hospital and the nurse whose anxious face wavered in and out of his vision. As polio gripped his weakened lungs more tightly with every labored breath, Marvin Moran thought desperately of his young wife and two small children, and of the unpaid mortgage on his home. This was no time for him to die!

Only a few days before, he had been on a singing tour in the Midwest—fatigued, but happy that his career was progressing so well. In the car on his way home, he developed a fever. It was nothing to worry about, he thought. But in a few more hours, he was to learn crushing news: *He had polio.*

"My legs had become immobile," he recalls. "Spinal polio had done its part. Then bulbar polio started knocking out the top part of my body. I could feel the paralysis taking over the nerves in my body as it moved closer to my head."

Each time that Marvin Morgan struggled for one more painful breath, his stomach cavity went into spasm. He had reached the crisis. The hush in the room was broken only by the in-sucking sound that indicated the approaching end of the singer's life.

"I knew I was dying," Moran said later. "I had been struggling to breathe for a day and a half. I was so exhausted, I couldn't fight any more."

Then came the most unbelievable moment of his life. Barely conscious, Moran murmured a simple prayer:

"God forgive me for my sins.

I put my soul in your hands."

Things began to happen—immediately. "As soon as I let God take over," Moran said, "I felt surrounded and cradled by warmth. I could sense God's presence. Suddenly, I had a vision. I saw my vocal teacher of many years before. He was teaching me how to breathe properly—using my diaphragm. He was showing me how to take short 'catch' breaths the way a batter does just before he hits the ball.

"I stopped gasping so deeply for air and used the 'catch' breath. To my amazement, it began to work. What a marvelous feeling! I began to breathe fairly well. The spasms were relieved. I had learned the secret of *relaxed power*, and it was keeping me alive."

The next two weeks were a living hell. It took fourteen days for the crisis to pass. But the doctors were amazed that the polio could go all the way to the bulb of his brain, then halt so suddenly but a breath away from death. It was certain now that the Milwaukee vocalist would live.

A grateful Moran told friends: "My recovery from polio shows the tremendous power of prayer. It is true that faith can move mountains."

Now a staggering challenge awaited him. He set out on the laborious, frustratingly slow process of regaining the use of his semiparalyzed body. The doctors agreed that he could never walk or sing again.

"But I was convinced that I would," Moran said. Long, tedious hours of speech and physical therapy followed. He had to completely rebuild his voice and his body. In time, he was braced so that he could sit up in bed. Then he progressed to a wheelchair—and mobility.

"I remember how I'd get into my wheelchair and go behind stage at the Veterans' Rehabilitation Hospital and practice my singing. My voice, nasal from the effects of polio, was awful. But I kept at it."

Only one year after Marvin Moran's battle with death, he limped out to home plate at the Milwaukee County Stadium and sang, "When Irish Eyes are Smiling." The capacity crowd responded with a thunderous ovation. Then he sang the

National Anthem—and 40,000 voices joined him. Although one arm hung motionless at his side, no one noticed; and on that August night in 1954, a new career began for Marvin Moran.

During the next ten years, Moran's melodic voice became a beloved part of the Braves' home games. He sang at the 1955 All-Star game and at both the 1957 and 1958 World Series. More than 14 million spectators heard him perform before he left the club in 1964.

"I loved every moment of it," he says. "Those days will always be happy memories for me."

Today Marvin Moran is a financial planner for the Northwestern Mutual Life Insurance Company. He fills numerous singing engagements, frequently conducting hymn sings throughout Wisconsin on Sunday evenings.

About his experience at the brink of death, Moran says, "God had a special plan for me. I am thankful that He has given me this opportunity to tell people of the wondrous power of prayer."

Her faith withstood even the most
terrifying name in the underworld. . .

"OF WHOM SHALL I BE AFRAID?"

by ALICE WELLMAN

It was January of 1931 and my engagement as soloist for Maestro Cherniavsky's Symphony Orchestra at the Saenger Theatre, a motion picture palace of New Orleans, would end in two weeks. I loved to sing and for the four-shows-a-day stretch I was paid $125 a week. This was a fortune! This was especially so for a missionary's child reared in the jungles of West Africa, who had earned her musical education and who hadn't owned more than one pair of stockings at a time, until she began to sing for a living six months ago.

But now I was obsessed by worry. Where would my next job come from? The depression was in full sway. In New York City, musical shows were few and seasoned performers were plentiful.

"Alice," yelled the stage manager as I came off stage. "A man's waiting to see you."

The man tipped his black hat and handed me a card which read: "Curly Stone, Booking Cafés and Picture Houses, 54 West Randolph Street, Chicago."

"They need a prima donna in a Chicago club called the Frolics," he said. "They want this girl singer to be a new face in Chicago. I can get you $150 a week."

I was awed by the salary. Of Chicago I knew nothing. I signed the contract and asked, "Who owns The Frolics?"

"Uncle Jakey's the manager." Curly Stone lit a big cigar. "Everybody calls him Uncle Jakey."

"Does he own it, too?"

"I'm personal representative for the club. We'll have a

bangup show this turn."

"But whom do I work for?" I persisted.

"What do you care? You'll get good money."

"I have to know before I pay my fare to Chicago. If anything goes wrong, I'll be stranded."

"Well," he grunted, "Uncle Jakey handles the club for Al Brown. You make good with this outfit and you'll be set for life."

On February 15, I opened at The Frolics on Chicago's South Side. It was an elaborate café and I was much impressed, particularly since I'd never even been in a nightclub before.

Three weeks later, I stood in the wings, watching the lineup of girls in exit from their opening number. Their faces shone with vivacity and their gorgeous legs pranced high and fast.

They ran to their dressing room, calling excitedly, "Al Brown's here! Al Brown's out front!"

I heard my entrance music. I was on. My finish song was the sobby torch hit, "Give Me Something to Remember You By." It brought an unexpected ovation. Bowing to the applause, I could see Uncle Jakey at the back of the club, looking at the tables on my left. I looked too.

Around a long table sat a group of perhaps thirty men, pounding their hands together. Blobs of faces, bodies relaxed yet taut. Like the sleepy jungle animals, I thought, ready for a sudden spring.

Three encores later, Uncle Jakey hailed me back stage. "Al Brown likes your work, kiddo," he said deferentially. "He wants you to come to his table."

"Good," I said. "Maybe he'll order me one of those good steak sandwiches."

We approached the long table. "Which one is Al Brown?" I asked.

Uncle Jakey looked at me questioningly, then pointed out the stocky man at the head of the table. The man's dark hair receded from a high forehead. A great scar cut down the side of his face.

Terror swept over me, buzzed in my ears, blurred my eyes. I had read the papers, seen this man's picture many times. "Al Brown" was his alias.

He rose. The others rose as if on signal. "Where'd such a little girl as you get that big sweet voice?" he rasped, smiling at me.

I couldn't speak but I was praying, silently pleading for help. Then the voice of my mother spoke as clearly as if she stood beside me. "The Lord is the strength of my life; of whom shall I be afraid?"

Al Brown turned to the impassive faces around him. "Meet my friends, babe. This is Nick. Frank. Joe . . .Max. . ." And so on down the line. "You'll join us after the show. We'll go to the hotel for drinks and eats." It was a command.

I wondered at the exact formation in which we walked the short blocks to the hotel. Al Brown and I moved within a solid phalanx of his men. Someone kicked a pebble and the man beside me jerked his hand out from beneath his coat. He had a revolver in it. Well, I was used to firearms. Papa always carried them in Angola because of the snakes and dangerous beasts.

Al Brown's rooms covered an entire floor of the hotel. Luxurious furnishings, refectory tables laden with delectable food, two bars from which liquors flowed into big heavy glasses. A burly man, his gun beside him, fed records into a Victrola.

"Ever had any Napoleon brandy?" Al Brown said to me.

"No," I answered. I'd never heard of it.

He led me into a small room to an elaborately carved table on which sat a dark bottle and two bellied glasses. Proudly, he showed me the label.

"But I don't drink," I said.

He stared unbelievingly at me. "Tell me about yourself, baby," he ordered. "Where were you raised?"

"In Chiyaka on Mount Elende in Angola."

"How'd you come to be there?"

"Mama and Papa took me there when I was six weeks old. They were missionaries. Papa was a doctor and Mama had a school for the Africans."

"Well, you got a new line, anyway," he said skeptically. "Who'd your father doctor?"

"Mostly lepers. But he researched a lot—on serums for snakebites. West Africa has two groups of poisonous snakes, the adders and the cobras. Papa worked on a polyvalent serum that would protect against both types of snakebite."

"Whew! *Nobody* could make that up." He leaned toward me. "I'd have been scared to death. Weren't you?"

"No. But Mama was frightened a lot. She was always

protecting us children from mosquitoes and tse-tse flies and scorpions and leopards. We lived in the leopard country. But she didn't let us be afraid."

"What'd she do?" He was curious.

"She always knelt down and prayed."

"So? Your mother still alive?"

"Yes. Mama lives in Wichita, Kansas. We lost Papa but I help my brothers take care of Mama now. She. . ."

Al Brown interrupted me with a kingly gesture. He pinched my cheek with his massive fingers. "Okay, baby," he said, turning to the door.

"Nick!" he roared. Nick, gun in hand, appeared instantly.

"Put this kid in Joe's taxi and tell him to drive her home. Safe."

The next evening, when I reached the club, Uncle Jakey handed me a small box from a well-known florist.

"For you, Alice," he said respectfully. The box held a corsage of three white orchids. I laughed delightedly for they were the first ones I'd ever received in a box. In the African rain forest, they grew on trees. Their centers were pushed open. Each held a folded hundred-dollar bill.

"Al Brown told me to deliver them to you personal," he said. "A message goes with them. The orchids are for you but the money's for your mother."

That night I wrote to my brother Paul. Paul was on the Kansas City *Star* and I thought he'd find the facts of mother's gifts amusing.

Two days later, Paul rapped on my hotel room door. "You're leaving Chicago," he said.

"But Paul, my contract—my salary?"

"Hurry and pack, honey," he said firmly. He put me on a plane that evening. Back in New York, I landed a job in an operetta, *not* a nightclub.

Since I sang in The Frolics twenty-eight years ago, I have seen Al Brown's name blazoned in headlines many times. I know there was one moment in his life, though he may never have recognized it, when he felt the power of prayer. And that was the moment when I learned the strength that came from the Lord, whether you faced the dangers of African jungles or worked for Al Capone in Chicago.

Henry J. Kaiser's wealth is great but
he learned the true values of life
from his mother. . .

THE MAN WHOSE WORK
WILL NEVER END

by W. CLEMENT STONE

I went to Hawaii for several reasons, one of which was to find true stories. I found one that had a terrific impact upon my future development—one that could also change the entire course of *your* life if you are ready.

It concerns the "common horse sense philosophy" of a man close to the top of the list of America's ten living men whose lives have been most beneficial to their country during peace and war, and who have generated great constructive forces to inspire men and women of future generations, *the man whose work will never end*—Henry J. Kaiser.

You know him by name—your future success would be assured if you could relate and assimilate into your own life his fundamentally effective philosophy. He continually proves that it works for *anyone who uses it.* He would like to share it with *you.* Regardless of your age, *you* can employ his formulas for success.

Today the wealth of the companies identified with his name have total assets of approximately one billion dollars—30 active corporations consisting of 125 plants in 20 countries which turn out over 300 products.

THE HAWAIIAN VILLAGE

I found my inspiring story there. The Hawaiian Village is the tourist's, artist's, philosopher's and author's dream come true of everything that Hawaii is and ought to be; Hawaiian music, singers, beautiful dancers; a white sand beach, six swimming pools and a lagoon, a yacht harbor with its catamarans and skiing facilities: palm-thatched guest houses, clusters of Waikiki Beach lanais, a 14-story hotel (the construction of additional hotels will ultimately accommodate four thousand guests at one time) in a Polynesian setting of acres of fragrant tropical gardens and palm trees where birds sing happily—all under a bright tanning sun during the day. Yet the dry air is cool in the shade; there is a covering of myriads of bright stars at night; and there is a monument to the needy in the form of a proposed ultra-modern hospital. There are facilities for conventions in the unique aluminum dome auditorium with a seating capacity of eighteen hundred persons.

More importantly, at the Hawaiian Village you feel that the brotherhood of man is a reality and not a theory. Europeans, Americans, Polynesians and Orientals meet on a plane of equality. They like and respect each other. There is magic in the air. Catholic and Protestant church services are held in the same church building, which is designed in the style of a native chief's longhouse.

A Hawaiian said to me, "Henry J. Kaiser inspires us. He has done more for Hawaii than anyone in our lifetime. He gives the young generation hope and courage. There was a time when no one dared compete with the 'Big 5' which had controlled these islands for generations. Henry J. Kaiser had the courage—he succeeded."

APPLIED IMAGINATION

In Henry J. Kaiser's workshop Robert C. Elliott, his executive assistant, said, "He first pictures in his mind what he wants; he tells one of our artists; the artist draws the picture; our architects lay out the plans; a date is set for construction; the work is completed. See for yourself. Here are the original pictures of the buildings in the Hawaiian Village; here are the photographs of the finished construction." Yes, Henry J. Kaiser uses applied imagination.

A SELF-EDUCATED MAN

Henry John Kaiser was born May 9, 1882 in Sprout Brook, New York, one of four children of Francis John Kaiser, a mechanic in a shoe factory, and Mary (Yopps) Kaiser, a practical nurse, both of whom were German immigrants.

At the age of thirteen he discontinued school and trudged

the sidewalks of New York, week after week, looking for work. He has always been inquisitive—he wanted to learn.   Like Thomas A. Edison, Andrew Carnegie and other self-made men he continued to learn after leaving school. He learned from experience—as a young salesman and a sales manager (perhaps the greatest vocation for any person interested in learning about people and interested in self-improvement) and he learned from history, literature, poetry and religious sermons.   He eagerly listens to the messages that are applicable to him!

For example, at the age of seventeen he was impressed by a sermon, the essence of which was "Cherish the rich memories of the smiles and sunshine you have given to others and the friendly smiles and sunshine that others have given to you."   At the age of nineteen, when he became an independent businessman, he put up a sign the size of a billboard over his store which read, "Meet the Man With a Smile."

He reacts to such inspirational writings, as these:

"Ah, but a man's reach should exceed his grasp, or what's a Heaven for?"

"All things are possible to him who has faith.   Because faith sees and recognizes the power that means accomplishment. Faith looks beyond all boundaries.   It transcends all limitations. It penetrates all obstacles. And it sees the goal. Faith never fails. It is a miracle worker."

"If thou canst believe, all things are possible to him that believeth."

" 'Tis the hardest thing in the world to give everything, even though 'tis usually the only way to get everything."

"What! Giving again? I ask in dismay, and must I keep giving and giving away? 'Oh, no,' said the angel looking me through, 'just keep giving till the Master stops giving to you.'"

NEVER GROW OLD

I predict that Henry J. Kaiser will live to celebrate more than his hundredth birthday. He himself says, "There are those who *never* grow old in mind and spirit and interest. How is it possible never to grow old, *really* old? By keeping young in all thinking, young in imagination, fresh in spirit, heart and soul. It *can* be accomplished!

"Mother used to say, 'Henry, be sure *you* practice what *you* preach.'" He does! He says, "Work! Put your life's plan into determined action and go after what you want with all that's in you!" He discovered from experience, "The person who makes fun and joy out of his work can leap out of bed at dawn and work with zeal; work becomes a habit."

Never grow old! At the age of forty-five, Henry J. Kaiser engaged in the $20 million project of building two hundred miles of highway with five hundred bridges in the interior of Cuba. It meant organizing six thousand workers and fighting serious obstacles. It was this vast project that crystallized his idea to employ the principle of the mastermind alliance. He shared this enterprise with other contractors through partnerships and associations; thus he developed the strength of combined knowledge, skill, capital and manpower. This principle is a most important ingredient in his formula for effectively building mammoth constructions with speed.

Kaiser's experience in Cuba made it easy for him to organize six large firms into a cooperative enterprise known as Six Companies, Incorporated. He became chairman of the executive committee. Through his guidance and experience were built the Hoover, Bonneville, Grand Coulee and Shasta Dams, the piers of the San Francisco Bay Bridge, levees on the Mississippi River, and pipelines throughout the Northwest, Southwest and in Mexico. At the age of fifty-seven, he founded the largest cement plant in the West, which was the second largest in the world.

Keep in mind that throughout his life when others said to him as they have to you, "It can't be done" he knocked out the "t" and said to himself, "It can be done!" And he did it.

Yes, never grow old. At about the age of sixty, during World War II, he built over one thousand five hundred ships with such rapidity that he startled the industry. He dared to think of new, fast methods to get results. He founded the first (and still the only) iron and steel plant on the Pacific Coast at Fontana, California. He built and operated two magnesium plants. He supplied all of the bulk cement used in the construction of our Pacific fortifications. He operated plants manufacturing aircraft parts, and he managed the largest artillery shell operations in the country.

THE MOST PRICELESS GIFT

Henry J. Kaiser inherited from his mother "the most price-less gift"—an inheritance that you or any father or mother might pray to give to your children. When Mary Kaiser was in her late thirties, after her day's work, she spent hours as a voluntary nurse helping the unfortunate. Often she said to her son, "Henry, nothing is ever accomplished without work. If I leave you nothing else but the *will to work*, I leave you *the most priceless gift*—the joy of work!"

"LOVE PEOPLE AND SERVE THEM"

"It was my mother," continued Mr. Kaiser, "who first taught me some of the greatest values in life—love of people and the importance of serving others. Mother was only forty-nine and I was sixteen when she died in my arms—died because of lack of medical care. The thought of my mother, or your mother or father, or children or loved ones dying prematurely when a doctor or a good hospital could save them—the thought of such needless sacrifice of human lives has always prodded me into action."

Hundreds of thousands of persons have received medical, surgical and hospital care at low cost. Others who suffered a speech paralysis can now talk. The crippled have been restored to useful lives in rehabilitation centers. All this has happened because of the inspiration of a mother who died in the arms of her son because she was too proud to ask for charity and too poor to pay for medical care—a mother who said to her son, "Love people and serve them." The Kaiser Foundation—a non-profit charitable trust—is only one of the monuments to her memory.

HUMAN RELATIONS

Henry J. Kaiser knows how to get along with people. Many feel that he has a genius for developing good relations with labor unions. He says, "The great truths by which to live are simple. The Sermon on the Mount and the Golden Rule are simple. I always try to stress the positive approach—down-to-earth attitudes that can succeed. Here are some of them:

"First—mutual acceptance, recognition and confidence in each other, secondly—honesty and integrity in our dealings together; thirdly—in bargaining, we must understand each other, not bog down in double-talk or demand lopsided victories."

PRAYER

In each of Henry J. Kaiser's speeches he utters a prayer. In the sincerity and spirit of the Man Whose Work Will Never End this article closes with a reverent prayer that Henry J. Kaiser will continue to live for many years and thus add additional momentum to the good work he has so ably started.

HOW TO BECOME THE PERSON YOU WANT TO BE
Henry J. Kaiser says:
1. "Know yourself and decide what you want most of all to make out of your life. Then write down your goals and a plan to reach them.
2. "Use the great powers you can tap through faith in God and the hidden energies of your sown and subconscious mind.
3. "Love people and serve them.
4. "Develop your positive traits of character and personality.
5. "Work! Put your life's plan into determined action and go after what you want with all that's in you."

Each man weighs his gifts from
God on a different scale. . .

"GOD HAS BEEN GOOD TO ME"

by R. M. GOOD

For 25 years I watched him fight cancer of the face. First, just a small speck that began to grow larger; then, year after year, I watched him go to the hospital and have a bit more cut out each time. As the years went by, his face was hardly a face at all as more and more was cut away. But always when he returned, with what was left of that face, he tried to smile and never once uttered a complaint or seemed to be downhearted.

He was a skilled mechanic and finished carpenter—recognized as the best in all the surrounding Ozark hills.

When he did a job he seemed to stand back and survey it to see if there was anything left out that could be added to make it as nearly perfect as possible. Then he would see some little place that the average person would pass up and he would be busy touching up this and that. Then, when he had done his best again, he would look it over and a smile of contentment would come over his face.

I suspect he often said to himself, "My work will be my face and my life." I doubt if he often looked in the mirror and noticed that damaged face where each day the cancer bit a mite deeper.

No matter how humble the home he worked in, or how small the job, or how crude the other work around and about, it never seemed to bother him at all. This was his work, and it had to be done right. He appeared never to give a glance at the work of others; a shoddy job done by someone else was not his concern. His own work seemed to be all that mattered. Nevertheless, I suspect when the job was done he had an inner sense of pride and joy when he saw how outstanding it was—but never once did I hear him boast about it.

As the years went by, he became weaker and weaker, his step was less sure, and his hands did not move with the confidence and speed that had so characterized him. He was unable to do many things he had done before. However, no matter what the work or pay, he always had an insatiable desire to do a good job.

The help he was able to get was not able to catch his vision; they thought he was cranky to try so hard to complete each and every detail. So more and more he worked alone. He did not complain or bitterly rail at the inefficiency of the other fellow. He would just appear the next morning by himself with no explanation of the absence of his helper.

During the latter days when he had only the shambles of a face, he would wrap it up in a red bandana handkerchief, leaving only his eyes showing.

When you met him on the street, there was always a cheery greeting. As time went on and he found it more and more difficult to say the words, often his greeting would be given with a move of his walking stick. This stick, too, was a thing of beauty, carved out by his skillful hands.

His life seemed to be filled with contentment and peace. I am sure many times he thanked God for those hands and for the fact that they were marred in no way.

He often would be missed about his usual haunts for weeks, or perhaps months, as he would make his journey to the hospital for the surgeon to cut away a little more. Then you would see him again—a bit more gruesome. There would be no complaint, no telling of his operation and the pain. He would just quietly go about the work that was always awaiting his return.

In all of this quarter of a century, I never knew him to come back with any complaints or mention in any way the pain. You would think there was nothing the matter if you did not see his face.

When his days of labor seemed to be coming to an end, his chief concern was that his tools might be in good hands. He sent for me one day and told me that he wished I would find for him some young man who would appreciate and properly use them.

When I took a young man to see him about the tools, there

came over his face a look of contentment and satisfaction. His work was finished and he was ready to cash in.

A few days before he died I went to see him. He was walking in the yard. His face was nearly completely covered with bandages and only his eyes were uncovered. As he hobbled about the yard, he said to me, "I am going to keep young just as long as I can."

The day he died I went to see him again. The odor in the room was so offensive you could hardly stay there. What was left of his face was a mass of scars and there was really no longer anything to cut away. You could tell he was in great pain and had many a sleepless night, but still there was no word of complaint.

I shall never forget his last words. Ever afterwards they have made me ashamed whenever I am inclined to complain. Still, day after day, they are vivid in my memory.

These words were: "God has been awfully good to me. I have never had any reason to complain."

*Poverty-stricken, paralyzed and rejected he still
presented the world with the greatest
oratorio ever written—*The Messiah . . .

HANDEL'S EASTER MASTERPIECE

by HENRY N. FERGUSON

On a cold winter night in 1741, an elderly stoop-shouldered man ambled listlessly along a dark London street. George Frederick Handel was starting one of the aimless, despondent wanderings which had become a nightly ritual for him. As he walked, his tortured mind flitted between the memories of past glories and the hopeless despair of the future. For four decades Handel had written music which had won him the adulation of the aristocracy of England and the Continent. The favorite of royalty, he had been showered with many honors. And then, abruptly, court society had turned on him. His once-famous operas were broken up by gangs of rowdies. It was only a matter of time until Handel was reduced to abject poverty.

A cerebral hemorrhage paralyzed his right side. He was unable to walk, move his right hand or write a note. Doctors could give him no hope for recovery.

The old composer went to Aix-la-Chapelle to take the baths. In spite of his doctor's warning that staying in the scalding waters longer than three hours at a time might kill him, Handel stayed in nine hours at a stretch. Gradually inert muscles took on new life. He began to walk, his hand lost its paralysis.

As his health returned, Handel began working again. In a frenzy of creativeness, he wrote four operas in quick succession. Again he found himself the recipient of many honors. And again the hand of fate struck him a cruel blow.

Queen Caroline, who had long been his patroness, died. Handel's income was immediately reduced. England found herself in the grip of such a bitter winter that fuel could not be wasted on heating the theaters. All engagements were canceled. Handel lived for a while on money borrowed from friends. As he sank deeper into debt, he lost his creative spark. He felt old, tired and hopelessly beaten.

On this night, as he tramped restlessly along a deserted street, he paused for a moment before the dark outline of a church. In bitter self-pity he pondered his situation. Why had God permitted his creativeness to be restored, only to let it be torn once more from his grasp?

Head bent against the sting of an icy wind, he made his way back to his humble room. As he pushed open the door he saw a package lying on the table. Tearing off the wrappings, he saw that it was the text of a musical composition. It was entitled *A Sacred Oratorio.*

Handel grunted contemptuously when he saw that it was from a second-rate poet, Charles Jennens. The note asked if Handel would start work immediately on the oratorio. A postscript added the information that "the Lord gave the Word."

Handel leafed indifferently through the oratorio. Suddenly a passage held his eye: "He was despised and rejected of men . . . He looked for someone to have pity on him, but there was no man; neither found He any to comfort Him."

A sense of kinship warmed Handel's heart. He read on. "He trusted in God . . . God did not leave his soul in Hell . . . He will give you rest."

The words, burning into his consciousness, began to take on meaning. "I know that my Redeemer liveth . . . Rejoice . . . Hallelujah."

The old fire that had inspired the rulers of Europe began to rekindle. Wondrous melodies bubbled up from the seething caldron of his mind. He grabbed a pen from the table and started writing. With unbelievable swiftness his notes filled page after page.

His manservant found him the next morning, still bent over his make-shift desk, still writing. Noiselessly he put down the breakfast tray and slipped quietly away. When he returned at noon, the tray had not been touched.

For days the old servant watched anxiously over his master.

Handel refused food. He wrote continuously. Sometimes he would pause, striding up and down, flailing the air with his arms. When he finished the triumphant climax to the "Hallelujah Chorus," tears were streaming down his cheeks. "I did think I did see all Heaven before me and the great God Himself!" he told his servant.

Handel labored like a man possessed for 23 days. Then he collapsed on his bed, exhausted, and slept for 17 hours. On his desk lay the score of the greatest oratorio ever written—*The Messiah*.

Really worried now, Handel's servant sent for the doctor. But before the physician arrived, the composer was sitting up, yelling for food. He eased his hunger pangs by wolfing down half a ham, washing it down with tankards of ale. Then he lit his pipe and joked with his amazed doctor.

Although Handel was sure he had composed a masterpiece, London wanted no part of it and so he took *The Messiah* to Ireland at the personal invitation of the Lord Lieutenant. Handel insisted that the proceeds of its performance must go to charity.

Arriving in Dublin, Handel lost no time merging two choirs and beginning rehearsals. So many tickets were sold for the first performance that notices were published in the newspapers begging the ladies not to wear their hoopskirts to the concert and the men to leave their swords at home. On April 13, 1742, crowds waited at the theater doors for hours before the opening. The response was tumultuous, even Handel was awe-struck by his creation.

After his Dublin triumph, London began begging to hear the work. It was during the first London performance that a strange thing happened. The audience, carried away by the power of the "Hallelujah Chorus" and following the King's example, arose in unison as though by a prearranged signal. Since then audiences the world over have expressed a similar respect by rising at the onset of this chorus and remaining standing until its conclusion.

For the remainder of Handel's life he presented *The Messiah* annually. All the proceeds went to the Foundling Hospital, and in his will he bequeathed the royalties from this work to the same charity.

Handel once more ran the gamut of misfortune, but never again did he permit despair to get the upper hand. Age robbed him of his vitality. He went blind, but his unflagging spirit never wavered.

On the evening of April 6, 1759—Handel was 74—he attended a performance of *The Messiah*. Suddenly he collapsed. He was taken home and put to bed. His spirit was still valiant, but the flesh was beginning to weaken. "I should like to die on Good Friday," he announced to his friends. And on April 13, the anniversary of the first presentation of *The Messiah*, in accord with his wish, the great composer's soul left his body forever.

For two hundred years now his spirit has gone marching on in *The Messiah*, an international symbol of the triumph of hope over despair. For the genius of his pen lighted a torch that has brought illumination to the dark places of the earth wherever there are voices to sing and hearts that beat with courage.

You have an "unseen partner" who will help you . . .

BREAK THE WORRY HABIT

by DR. NORMAN VINCENT PEALE

Nobody does good work who tugs and strains and is rigid about it. "Easy does it" is the proper method.

The person who works the easiest does the most in the shortest time and his work shows the mark of skill. Don't live and work the hard way. We suggest that you study and master the following rules for making your work easy.

1.   Drop the idea that you are Atlas carrying the world on your shoulders. The world would go on even without *you*. Don't take yourself so seriously.

2.   Tell yourself that you like your work. It may be difficult to make yourself believe that, for you may have talked yourself into hating it. Or you may be a "fighter of the job," that is to say, you struggle against it rather than with it. This emphasis on liking your job will tend to make it a pleasure instead of a drudgery. Perhaps you do not need to change your job. Change yourself and your work will seem different.

3.   Plan your work for today and every day, then work your plan. Lack of system produces that "I'm swamped" feeling. To arrange work in an orderly way, and perform it in the same manner, makes the total job infinitely easier.

4.   Decide that you will not try to do everything at once. That is why time is spread out. Repeat the wise advice from the Bible, "This *one* thing I do." Say that to yourself *now*, three times, emphasizing the word *one*. One step at a time will get you there much more surely than haphazardly leaping and jumping. It is the steady pace, the consistent speed that leads most efficiently from start to destination.

5.   Practice becoming expert in correct mental attitudes,

remembering that ease or difficulty in your work depends upon *how* you think about it. Think it is hard, and it is hard. Think it is easy, and it is easy.

6. Determine now to restudy your job for "Knowledge is power" (over your job). It is always easier to do a thing right. Make your own job analysis to discover more right ways of doing things. The right way is right because it meets less resistance and is therefore easier than the wrong way.

7. Practice being relaxed about your work. Again remind yourself that "Easy always does it." Do not press or strain. Take your work in your stride. One way to do this is to repeat such a work formula as the following: "I can handle this job. I know this material or this business. I am well informed about it and am competent to deal with it; therefore, I will have no fear or nervousness about it and besides, God is with me to help me." This will give you a feeling of peace and confidence and you can do the job in a relaxed frame of mind.

8. Discipline yourself not to put off until tomorrow what you can do today. Accumulations make the job harder than it actually is or should be. Do not drag yesterday's burdens along with you. Keep your work up to schedule. Spend a minute *now* listing the things to do today, and tomorrow, and the next day. This will immediately relieve today's burden, for usually you do not need to do so much right now as you nervously think you do. If your mind gets the idea that you have too much to do, it immediately accepts tired thoughts, your energy drops, and the job becomes heavy and hard.

9. Pray about your work, today's work. You will get some of your best ideas that way. Never start a day or any job without praying about it.

10. Take on the "unseen partner." It is surprising the load He will take off you. God is as much at home in offices, factories, shops, as in churches. Do not spurn God's help, for He has broad shoulders and strong arms and wonderful ideas. All are available to you. He knows more about your business than you do. His help will make your work easy.

A bright light guides your
path to success when you adopt . . .

A LIVING PHILOSOPHY

by W. CLEMENT STONE

The essence of a living philosophy is that it must be alive. To be alive, it must be lived, you must act! Actions, not mere words, determine the validity of a man's living philosophy.

For faith without works is dead.

Whether he recognizes it or not, everyone has a philosophy. You become what you think. Now my living philosophy is:

First, God is always a good God.

Secondly, truth will always be truth, regardless of lack of understanding, disbelief or ignorance.

Thirdly, man is the product of his heredity, environment, physical body, conscious and subconscious mind, experience and particular position and direction in time and space . . . and something more, including powers know and unknown. He has the power to affect, use, control, or harmonize with all of them.

Fourthly, man was created in the image of God, and has the God-given ability to direct his thoughts, control his emotions and ordain his destiny.

Fifthly, Christianity is a dynamic, living, growing experience. Its universal principles are simple and enduring. For example, the Golden Rule, "Do unto others as you would have others do unto you," is simple in its concepts and enduring and universal in its application. But it must be applied to become alive.

Sixthly, I believe in prayer and the miraculous power of prayer.

Now what does this philosophy mean to me? It wouldn't

mean a thing unless I lived it. To live it, I must apply it. And therefore I shall give you an illustration of how I apply it in a time of need. Then it may be more meaningful to you.

In 1939 I owned an insurance agency which represented a large Eastern accident and health insurance company. Over a thousand full-time licensed agents were operating under my supervision in every state in the United States. My contract was verbal and provided for exclusive distribution of a specified series of accident policies. Under this working agreement, the business was owned by me. The company printed the policies and paid the claims. I assumed all other expenses.

It was spring. My family and I were vacationing in Florida when I received a letter from one of the chief executive officers of the company. This letter was brief: It stated that my services would be terminated at the end of two weeks; my license to represent the company, and the licenses of all my representatives, would be cancelled on that date; no policies could be sold or renewed after that date; and the president of the company was leaving on a trip and couldn't be reached for two months.

I was faced with a serious problem. The type of contract I had just wasn't being made any more. A new connection for a national operation such as mine within two weeks was an improbability. The families of the one thousand representatives who worked for me would also have a problem if I didn't find a solution.

Now what do you do when you have a serious personal problem—a physical, mental, moral, spiritual, family, social or business problem?

What do you do when the walls cave in?

What do you do when there is no place to turn?

That's the time your faith is tested. For faith is mere daydreaming unless applied. While true faith is applied continuously, it is tested at the time of your greatest need.

Now what would you have done if you had been faced with my problem? Here's what I did:

I told no one, but cloistered by myself in my bedroom for 45 minutes. There I reasoned that God is always a good God; right is right; and with every disadvantage there is a greater advantage if one seeks and finds it.

Then I kneeled down and thanked God for my blessings: a healthy body, a healthy mind, a wonderful wife and children, the privilege of living in this great land of freedom and unlimited opportunity, and the joy of being alive. I prayed for guidance. I prayed for help. And I believed that I would receive them.

And I did get into positive mental action!

On arising I began to engage in thinking time. Four resolutions were made:

1. I wouldn't be fired.
2. I would organize my own accident and health company and by 1956 would have the largest company of this kind in the United States.
3. By 1956 a specific objective would be reached. It was of such magnitude and so personal that it would be improper to mention it here; and
4. I would reach the president of the company regardless of what part of the world he might be in.

And then I got into physical action. I left the house and drove to the nearest public telephone booth to try to talk to the company president. I succeeded because I tried. The president was a kindly, understanding man of principle. He gave me permission to continue operations upon my agreement to withdraw from the state of Texas where the general agents of the company were having some competitive difficulties with my representatives. We were to meet at the home office in 90 days.

We did meet in 90 days. I am still licensed for that company and continue to give it business.

When 1956 came, the company I organized in 1939 was not the largest accident and health company in the United States. But it was the world's largest stock company writing accident and health insurance exclusively. My specific personal objective had also been achieved.

Now, what do you do when you have a serious personal problem—a physical, mental, moral, spiritual, family, social or business problem? Your philosophy will determine your answer.

Remember: the essence of a living philosophy is that it must be alive. To be alive, it must be lived. To be lived, you must act! Actions, not mere words, determine the validity of a man's living philosophy.

3
IDEAS UNLIMITED

Ideas control the world.
—James A. Garfield

They used logic, planted tin cans and
innocently waited for the harvest.

LOGIC AND THE UNKNOWN

by W. CLEMENT STONE

A small glass-bottomed boat approached the sandy beach of Rum Point on Grand Cayman Island in the British West Indies. Gleason, the native skipper, stopped at a coral reef . . . put on his skindiving helmet . . . checked his spear gun . . . dove into the water and swam among the coral rocks. Within six minutes he brought up five lobsters, three red snappers and three conch shells.

Conch salad properly seasoned . . . fresh, tender, juicy lobster boiled in salt water . . . snapper wrapped in aluminum foil and cooked over an open fire on the beach—what a lunch! And the conversation among the five of us was fascinating, informative and inspiring, too. For I'm a good listener—always searching for stories of true life experiences.

Dr. Curtis Bowman, a well-known Chicago surgeon, related his African experiences and those of his wife, Martha B. Bowman, author of the fascinating book *Ebony Madonna.* Here's part of the conversation:

"It was when we were in the East Belgian Congo that a wife of a missionary asked her houseboy, who had been with the family six years, 'What are you doing with the empty tin cans you take away each evening?'

" 'Don't you know?' was the reply.

" 'No, but I would like to. Please tell me. Just why do people buy them?'

" 'They buy them to use the same as you do,' the boy replied after some hesitation and with apparent amazement.

" ' I don't really understand. Won't you please tell me exactly what is done with the tin cans or how they are used?' the wife asked. And she was amazed when she heard his answer. I know I was. You will be, too. And here's his answer:

" 'When we get our freedom, we'll be rich. We'll have everything the white man has. Now we plant the tin cans . . . we bury them deep. Some day we too will grow automobiles.'"

I commented: "He reasoned logically from what his experience had taught him. For throughout his young life, he had seen beautiful flowers, edible crops and great trees grow from the ground. It seemed reasonable to him and his customers that tin cans, properly planted, would grow automobiles. But his reasoning, like that of many of us, was based on the wrong premises. For he didn't consider the *unknown*."

Dr. Bowman then told us of some of his experiences in learning about Africa.

"You see, my brother-in-law was a missionary in Africa for many years. With his instruction and help, we traveled from one mission to another—fifty-one mission stations in all. We talked the language of the missionary. The natives trusted us. They wanted to help us. We were well received everywhere. Although taking pictures of native dances is taboo, we were given the privilege to do so."

"In *Ebony Madonna* your wife tells a fascinating story of a native with leprosy who returned to his own village when cured. The natives didn't believe leprosy was curable and reacted accordingly. What about leprosy? What about the cures?" I asked.

"Africa has millions suffering from leprosy." And then he told me the thrilling, exciting experiences of Dr. Carl Kline Becker of Oicha Hospital, Oicha Buna, Congo.

"An average of twelve hundred patients a day are treated by Dr. Becker and his staff besides the more than twenty-eight hundred in his leper colony. Ninety per cent of the patients are cured. Of course, if an arm is eaten away, a new one is not grown, but the disease is arrested and the patient is permanently cured."

As you have seen: The missionary's houseboy used logic, but the truth of how automobiles come into existence was *unknown to him . . .* he was ignorant of the facts. The cure of the dreaded disease leprosy is even today *unknown to millions.* Yet 90 per cent of patients are cured in the leprosarium. One hundred per cent can be cured if given medical attention in time.

So in reasoning, let's *start with what we do know;* use logic; but before coming to conclusions, let's reckon with the *importance of the unknown.* For: *Truth will be truth regardless of any person's ignorance, disbelief or refusal to try to understand.*

Meet an employer who advocates
reading on the job and thinking with
your feet—on the desk.

READ AND RELAX FOR PROFIT

by CLAIRE COX

What would your boss do if he found you tilted back in your chair, feet upon your desk, reading a book or magazine on company time?

Would he fire you?

Not if your boss was Norman L. Cahners, millionaire inventor, innovator and chairman of the board of the Cahners Publishing Company—and if you were reading something to help you in your work.

Cahners, a robust man with an easy smile not only has *no* objection to putting feet on desks and reading at work; he encourages both.   Early in his highly successful publishing career, which was launched with an invention that helped win World War II, Cahners, now forty-five, realized that one of the secrets of being a good employer was in practicing what you preach. What is right for the boss, he concluded, is right for his employees. Men and women like to work for a person who encourages them to forge ahead.

This employer likes to sit back with his feet on his desk. He also believes in reading at work, if the material is pertinent. So enthusiastic is he about both, in fact, that he has launched a campaign for on-the-job reading programs throughout business and industry to increase efficiency at work and relaxation at home.

Being an idea man, Cahners has made his own foot-on-desk reading periods as comfortable as he can. He did it by inventing a special footrest. When he wants to think, dictate or read, he pulls out the top drawer of his desk in his peaceful, uncluttered, seventh-floor Boston office, places a small footrest on it, leans back and swings his feet into position. He may look as if he is taking it easy, but he maintains that some of his most constructive work is done in this restful posture.

"Employers should encourage on-the-job reading," he says, "as long as it has something to do with the work. To keep abreast of developments, it is difficult to read at home, what with the competition from television and other distractions."

To illustrate how complicated the reading problem can be, Cahners has listed 2,160 technical and industrial publications in this country alone. There were 1,800 in 1949—and only 10 in 1850. The total circulation of all such publications last year was more than 43 million—with far more actual readers.

"The technical man never stops working," Cahners explains. "His leisure time and shorter working hours give him more time—more time for homework from work and it is increasing every day."

Cahners, by being what Madison Avenue calls "a thinking man," has solved his own problems on this score. He supervises the publication of fourteen industrial and trade magazines, serves as a corporation director, engages in a number of philanthropic activities and still finds time to putter around his suburban Brookline, Massachusetts, home with his wife and three children and engage in his favorite pastime—sailing off Bar Harbor, Maine.

Ever since he can remember, Cahners has been a man in a hurry. At Harvard, he set a record of 9.3 seconds for the 100-yard dash that no one has been able to beat. He was a member of a U.S. Olympic track team after he graduated from Harvard in 1936, and still is remembered at Harvard for his prowess on the football field.

Born to a well-established family, Cahners attended Phillips Academy at Andover, Massachusetts, graduating in 1932. He is a member of the Andover Alumni Council, where his pet interest is in setting up scholarships so poor but worthy boys can attend the famous Ivy League prep school.

Cahners always has worked for himself—except for his hitch in the Navy. His first job after college was selling furniture on the installment plan to rural New Englanders. Before long, he had several hundred persons stumping the countryside for him. He learned quite a bit about merchandising on that job—enough to win him a naval decoration later and start him on the road to bigger things.

The day after Pearl Harbor was attacked, Cahners decided not to wait for his draft board to call him. He left his job and enlisted in the Navy. Because of his experience in moving furniture from factory to home, he was assigned to try to help solve the huge wartime problem of getting supplies to the fighting men.

What did Cahners do? He went into action—Cahners style— by sitting back, putting his feet on his desk and pondering. The result was a series of highly technical but unusually workable innovations, including the use of a pallet contraption that became the standard wartime shipping platform for everything from ammunition to chocolate bars.

The Navy awarded Cahners a special citation. Then, at official request, he wrote a publication on war matériel handling. It was a Navy periodical, but request for copies streamed in from civilian manufacturers.

This is what really set Cahners, the old track star, into high speed. After he left the service, he received official naval approval to convert his Navy publication to peacetime use. He changed "matériel" to "materials" in a new magazine called *Modern Materials Handling,* which he gave away to persons he thought should have it, letting the advertisers foot the bills. By using that magazine as a foundation, he has built a publishing empire.

In the course of expanding his activities, Cahners gave himself—and Western Union—a boost by using the telegraph company's facilities to make surveys of regular readers and seek new ones. This was so successful that Western Union now has an entire department devoted to making special canvasses for businesses.

Cahners hopes to bring his two sons into his business with him, but one of them is such a chip-off-the-old-rugged-individualist-block that he wants to branch out on his own. Both boys attend Andover, but Cahner's dream for both of them to be

Harvard men will not be realized.

As the fourteenth member of his family to attend Harvard, Cahners naturally wanted to make it unanimous with Robert, who is seventeen, and Andrew, who is fifteen. But Robert has his own ideas. Being independent he made his own college arrangements and will enter Dartmouth in the fall.

Robert wants to be a publisher, but of his own periodicals, not his father's.

Andrew has not made up his mind yet, but is following in his father's footsteps in at least one respect. He is already a track star at Andover though still only a freshman.

The third Cahners child is nine-year-old, red-haired Nancy, described by her doting father as "the light of my life."

Mrs. Cahners, the former Helene Rabb, is a charming woman who shares her husband's love of people and working with them. She is president of the Beth Israel Hospital women's auxiliary in Boston.

This full-time, nonpaying job includes two secretaries and an office staff. At thirty-nine, Helene Cahners is the youngest president ever to serve the 8,300-member organization.

As is the case with many a wife, Mrs. Cahners had to bide her time for quite a while before getting her first mink coat. Her husband, who admits to being economical despite the fact that he is a millionaire, explains why. "I had to sit with my feet on my desk and think about it for a while first," he says.

4

LOVE UNLIMITED

*To love is to place our happiness in
the happiness of another.*
—Gottfried von Liebnitz

TO ANY LITTLE BOY'S FATHER

There are little eyes upon you
And they're watching night and day;
There are little ears that quickly
Take in everything you say.

There are little hands all eager
To do everything you do;
And a little boy who's dreaming
Of the day he'll be like you.

You're the little fellow's idol;
You're the wisest of the wise.
In his little mind, about you
No suspicions ever rise.

He believes in you devoutly,
Holds that all you say and do,
He will say and do in your way,
When he's grown up, just like you.

There's a wide-eyed little fellow
Who believes you're always right;
And his ears are always open
And he watches day and night.

You are setting an example
Every day in all you do;
For the little boy who's waiting
To grow up and be like you.

—Anonymous

He discovered a symbol of
true love when he read . . .

THE LETTER ON
YELLOW SCRATCH PAPER

by W. CLEMENT STONE

The cab driver and I became quite friendly as we conversed together while riding from Kennedy Airport to uptown New York last Monday.

You see, I try always to make a cab trip in New York pay off with a human interest story. And this trip was no exception.

"Tell me about yourself and some of your experiences," I suggested. So Louis, the cab driver, told me of a strange experience he had had the previous week. And when he did, I felt he was ready—ready to talk about himself and his family. So I directed his mind in the desired channel with the question: "Are those your four children?" referring to a picture on the dashboard in front of the steering wheel. "Yes," he answered, "they are wonderful kids. We have a lot of fun together." And he kept talking.

By the time we were within a few blocks of my destination, I sensed that he had an inner urge to share with me something very personal to him. And now I share it with you; a symbol of love—a letter written on yellow scratch pad paper.

He had already shown me his wallet with a picture of his wife when she was a bride and colored snapshots of the children. He had a loving word to say about each.

Now he handed me the letter. It was from his wife. She had handed it to him when she kissed him as he left the front door that morning.

"I suppose in every marriage there are arguments from time to time," he started. Then continued, "My wife and I had what some might call a family squabble last night. She was griping about our early marriage—when the children were younger, telling me how other husbands helped around the house and I did nothing.

"Said she, 'My brother Herman always helped Helen when the children were young. He would wash the dishes, even scrub the floors. And Irene's husband, Tom, would make necessary repairs to the furniture—he'd even change the baby's diapers and never complain. But you—you weren't helpful at all when the children were young. You weren't a good father then.'

"You see," he apologized to me, "as a cab driver I worked twelve hours a day. And my job was to make the money. I made good money because I made every hour count. Then when I got home, I was tired. I needed sleep and some relaxation.

"And look what we have to show for it," he continued. "A home of our own in Queens, a good Chevy car, life insurance, some money in the bank and a summer home in upstate New York. In the summer the family is on the lake. I spend Fridays, Saturdays and Sundays with them. Because they are away, I work an extra four hours Mondays, Tuesdays, Wednesdays and Thursdays."

I began to read the letter and as I did so I felt the emotions of its writer. Now you will feel it too because of the love and sincerity with which it was written. For the following is part of what I read:

"I was wrong in finding fault with you. I was dead wrong in complaining about what you didn't do when the children were younger. I am humiliated that I complained you weren't a good father then. For I know of no husband or father that is more loving, kind and thoughtful of his children and wife. You are certainly doing the right thing for all of us.

"And it was wrong for me to allow my feeling of the past to interfere with our happiness now. For we do have a happy home. And now it is I who, with faultfinding and nagging, have brought unhappiness to you.

"I love you so very much. I have the most wonderful husband in the world. And my children have a most loving and kind father. I hope you will forgive me."

And as I handed the yellow page back to Louie, he said, "This letter: It will never be forgotten. For I will keep it forever."

*Christmas, from now on, will have
a deeper meaning for you after
you understand . . .*

KELLEY'S CHRISTMAS GIFT

by OG MANDINO

The month of December was cold and wet and gloomy in England in 1944. Although the tides of war had shifted in favor of the Allies, our casualties still continued high so our morale matched the weather.

Our B-24 airbase, fifty miles north of London, was just like a hundred others spread carelessly over the face of England and we were similar to all the others in planes and personnel with one exception—we had Kelley.

I don't remember his first name but I do recall he was a navigator . . . and a good one. Kelley had habits that set him apart from most of us who assumed a phony air of boldness to hide our fear. For one thing he was older than most of us . . . probably near thirty. When we went to London every two weeks and raised unholy hell he remained behind and wrote letters to his wife, his mother, his son and every other relative whose address he kept in a little brown book. A forty-eight hour pass to Kelley meant stuffing his duffel bag with candy bars and canned food and bringing it to poor families in the village. Before each mission Kelley attended chapel services while most of us slept those extra fifteen minutes. Yes, to many of us, Kelley was a strange guy.

Then, about two weeks before Christmas, Kelley got an idea. He decided that we would throw a Christmas party on our base for all the British kids that lived in the area. He sold the idea to our Colonel and then he assigned projects to all of us. It was difficult to say no to Kelley . . . and when we weren't flying missions we had plenty of time on our hands anyway.

Kelley set up collection boxes inside the Post Exchange and I painted signs that asked for contributions of candy bars, chewing gum, canned fruit and cookies from each man's weekly allotment purchase. We filled dozens of boxes.

Then Kelley coaxed the mechanics on the flight line to make toys from spare parts and scrap metal. The carpenters got into the act and began building toy carts and crude rocking horses and even the nurses made stuffed dolls and animals. Everyone became involved and Kelley kept the whole operation coordinated in a way that would have made General Motors proud.

Two days before Christmas, the mess hall began to look like Macy's warehouse . . . and Kelley was all smiles . . . until someone reminded him that we had no Christmas ornaments or lights to hang. He solved this problem as swiftly as he solved the others. He commandeered boxes of silver chaff that we dropped during our bombing missions to confuse the enemy radar . . . and we had our "icicles." He had the base electrician wire a couple of hundred spare wing-tip lights to heavy cable and we spent a morning coloring them with paint that he produced from Lord knows where.

On Christmas eve we decorated the mess hall and although it was no Rockefeller Plaza we were all proud of our handiwork . . . even though none of us would admit it. On the way back to our barracks we got the "good news." We were flying a mission on Christmas Day. You can imagine the remarks next morning before, during and after the briefing. We were all thinking the same thing . . . what a day to die! Our mission, of course, wasn't going to affect the Christmas party. The base personnel all had their instructions from Kelley and all the buses from the motor pool had been assigned a special town or hamlet where they were to go to pick up the children.

When we returned on Christmas afternoon, from what had been a rough mission, we hurriedly changed clothes and dashed to the mess hall as soon as de-briefing was finished. The place was bedlam. It looked like recess time at my old grammar school. Kids were pushing their new carts and toy trucks, little girls skipped and danced with their new stuffed dolls clutched tightly to their breasts, while boys ran from one end of the hall to the other holding their miniature planes and imitating the sounds of Spitfires and P-51's. Every smiling face was smeared with chocolate . . . many for the first time ever. The wing-tip lights blinked overhead in multi-colored joy and someone had found a phonograph which was playing tinny but recognizable Christmas carols. I watched for a few moments remembering many happy childhood Christmases of my own. Then I left and slowly walked back to my barracks. In the distance someone gunned all four motors of a B-24, drowning out the joyous shouts from the hall.

I passed the chapel and then I stopped. Without even knowing what I was doing I found myself walking back up the cobblestone walk and pulling open the metal door.

I stepped inside for the first time since I had been on the base. The outside world quieted down. I felt myself kneeling and before I could stop myself I was sobbing. It was the first time I had cried since my mother had died. Finally I prayed . . . prayed for Kelley and the rest of his crew whose plane I had watched explode into flames after taking a direct hit only a few hours ago.

Since that Christmas, so many years ago, I never hear a Christmas carol or watch a child open a Christmas gift without remembering Kelley and counting my own blessings. Why Kelley is not here to enjoy each Christmas like the rest of us is a question I stopped asking myself . . . I finally realized that Kelley's gift to all of us was the same priceless gift of sacrifice and love that we all received from Him whose birthday we celebrate on Christmas Day.

She was a stranger and he
nearly rejected her request . . .

AND THEN THERE WAS LIGHT

by EARL STOWELL

Just a favor—granted almost grudgingly—changed my whole life. And because of that favor, in thousands of homes special lamps are lighted every night in unknowing tribute to a man whose name I do not know and to a woman's love for that man.

These lamps bring a warm glow to ranch houses at the very end of the electrical lines in Arizona. They press against the probing cold in rude farm houses in Idaho. They light tiny homes of coal or copper miners in Utah. They sit on tables in the homes of the humble, the well-to-do and the wealthy across America. They are treasured because each is handmade by someone in the family or by a friend. The sparkling beauty of the lamp is a constant reminder of that person's achievement.

Few know the story of the lamp.

Shortly after the Second World War, I was quietly going broke in a plastic-novelty manufacturing business. I had reached a state of numbness, where all I could do was work, snatch a few hours sleep and work again—doing work I could no longer afford to pay others to do.

This particular afternoon, annoyance swept over me when a woman, in her mid-thirties and very pale, entered the plant and put a cardboard box on the counter. Her eyes focused somewhere above my head. Words came in spurts like handfuls of confetti thrown at me. She wanted me to complete a pair of lamps for her.

Almost rudely, I said that I was running a factory, that I never did fix-it work. She didn't hear, for her words kept flicking out at me. I began to realize that her words had been rehearsed so many times that once started they had to keep tumbling over each other until they all came out.

She was trembling. I began to listen.

"I . . . I could pay . . . 50 cents each week. He left nothing . . . except these lamps . . . and . . . he couldn't even finish them for me."

Her fingers were white where she gripped the edge of the counter. A great shuddering sigh took complete possession of her. She fought for breath and went on. "He . . . did want to finish them . . . before . . ." She stopped for a moment. "Friends are getting me a job. It won't pay much. But I'll be able to pay 50 cents a week. I don't care for how long. Charge anything." Tears began to flow down her cheeks.

Suddenly I was very small, very humble.

I looked in the box. The pattern of the lamps was evident, just plastic blocks to be piled up until the stack was high enough. A larger piece was to act as the base, smaller pieces for feet. My own voice wasn't under perfect control. I kept my eyes on the box.

"There's plenty of plastic here—some extra. At least enough to pay for the work." I forced my eyes to meet hers.

For a moment she swayed; the effort had drained her. She steadied herself and uttered a single word.

"When?"

"Wednesday."

She wheeled around. As the door shut behind her, "Thank you—may God bless . . . ." floated back.

I avoided working on the lamps. What did I know about making lamps? Besides, wouldn't I just be making something that would only remind her of her pain? I couldn't afford the time. Time was money; I had little of either.

It was Tuesday afternoon before I dumped the blocks out on the workbench. I hated that pile of plastic. I picked up one piece and began to grind and polish it. Suddenly I was riding the feeling of anticipation. The rough-cut blocks began turning into diamond-like pieces of polished crystal. I slowed down for the first time in months, took my time, enjoyed watching each block become perfect under my fingers.

Then I drilled a hole through each block and threaded them on a pipe nipple that was to hold them together and carry the electric wires. I added the base and the feet and set the lamp on the bench. Then I knew why I had dreaded the job. The lamp that should mean so much to the widow looked just like what it was—a pile of plastic blocks. I felt a little sick.

Then, almost as if someone asked, I wondered, "Suppose I turned every other block a quarter-turn?" Almost automatically I loosened the nuts on the nipple and shifted the blocks. It was magic. That pile of blocks was transformed into a beautiful crystal lamp fit to go into any home. With a feeling that approached reverence, I assembled the second lamp and placed it beside the first. A glow seemed to surround them.

On Wednesday, I found myself anticipating the woman's return. It seemed a long time before she walked timidly toward the door. She hesitated for a moment in the shade of the giant tree that blocked the sky from the window.

As she entered, I picked up one lamp in each hand and set them before her. My eyes were fixed on hers. I wanted her to like those lamps—to really like them. But I wasn't prepared for the look of amazement that captured her face.

My eyes followed hers and I caught my breath.

A single piercing ray of bright sunlight had fought its way through the big tree outside the window. With pinpoint accuracy it struck the top of the nearest lamp. From there the light dripped from block to block, twisting, turning, reflecting as it went, making each polished surface burn with a pure white fire. The corners of the blocks acted as prisms, shattered the light and cast rainbows on the ceiling and down the walls.

As the tree branch moved back and forth, the ray of light struggled for freedom, only to be trapped in the lamp again and again. The whole room held something unreal.

She raised questioning eyes to mine. I nodded. A sudden sob shook her whole body. She gathered the lamps to her breast. "Thank . . . thank. . . ." she choked and stumbled out the doorway. She made her way unsteadily to a car where someone waited for her.

A few weeks later the day came when the long months of overwork demanded their due from me. Four doctors, one after another, looked wise, shook their heads and said, "Subarachnoid hemorrhage. If you recover, you must never work more than four hours a day."

When I got out of the Veterans' Hospital, my business was gone. The dollars I had left wouldn't even buy a good lawn mower. Tangible assets were a few hundred dollars' worth of plastics, a small stock of cements and dyes. I had not been in the area long enough to establish roots that could nurture me at such a time. How could I support my family?

Then I thought of high-school students and their crafts classes. At a nearby high school, I asked for and received permission to demonstrate the working of plastic. I explained how to cut, shape and polish it. A student spoke up.

"That looks like fun, but what could we make of it?"

Hopefully I looked at the instructor. He shrugged.

"What can we make of it?"

I wasn't prepared for the question. Then, I sensed—rather than saw—the glowing lamps. I sketched a lamp on the blackboard. The instructor liked it. He bought half my plastic. A few more calls and my stock was gone.

Do you ever wonder if the big companies in America have a heart?

Back home, I wrote four letters. I pulled no punches. I simply stated my condition; questionable physical condition, no money, no assured market, only an idea. I sent one to a plastic manufacturer (probably one of the largest American companies), one to a manufacturer of metal lamp parts, one to a cement and dye manufacturer, and one to a lamp socket company.

The first three answered at once. They offered 90-day credit on more supplies than I needed. I bought lamp sockets at the dime store as I needed them.

Then a difficulty: Plastic was too expensive for schools to keep much on hand. I remembered how the first lamps had come to my shop in rough cut form. I cut parts for a hundred lamps and wrapped them with the necessary lamp fittings in separate packages. I offered these kits to the schools.

That started it. I was soon busy cutting and delivering lamp kits.

Yes, thousands of students and adults will light these lamps tonight. Thousands of lamps will burn in tribute to a woman's love—and to a man who wanted to finish a pair of lamps so that the woman he loved would not have to move in darkness.

Love often reflects itself in a
promise made—and a promise kept . . .

"AND THEY LIVED
HAPPILY EVER AFTER"

by W. CLEMENT STONE

"Daddy, you promised to read me a story."

That's what Lou Fink heard his four-year-old son Kent say. It was late Friday evening. Lou had arrived home from the office too late to have dinner with Kent. And Lou hadn't bothered to call Peg. Peg, like thousands of housewives and mothers, worried while she waited as the minutes, and then the hours passed by.

"The streets are slippery. He may have had an auto accident. Certainly Lou could have called," Peg thought. Peg didn't like the uncertainty, and she didn't like worrying.

But now that Lou was home, he could listen to Kent's prayers and then put him to bed. She could salvage the roast from the oven. So Peg went to the kitchen while Lou carried Kent to his bedroom.

"Daddy, will you tell me a story?"

"Daddy will tell you a story tomorrow night," Peg called out.

"Daddy, last night you promised that if I went to sleep right away you would tell me a story tonight. And I did go to sleep right away. You promised me, Dad. You promised me."

Lou looked at Kent and said, "A promise is a promise, and a deal is a deal. Always remember that son."

So Lou began to tell Kent the fairy tale of the six-year-old boy who was a friend to all the animals in the forest. He knew each of them by name, and he could speak their language. For he understood them and they understood him. And all this was possible because the boy had magical powers. But he had these powers only so long as he lived up to his promises.

Now, before Lou arrived at that part of the fairy tale where the young boy broke a promise to himself and consequently lost his magical powers, Kent fell asleep. He was tired. And perhaps the story had had a sleepy effect on Lou as well, for Lou himself was asleep when Peg awakened him and said: "Dear, dinner is ready. It may be burnt, but it's late and I'm half starved. I didn't stop for lunch today."

A promise is a promise and a deal is a deal kept flashing through Lou's mind as he and Peg chatted during their dinner. And that is quite understandable. For a great fairy tale has deep roots that reach into the subconscious mind.

After dinner Lou pushed his chair away from the table slightly, lit a cigar and said: "Did you know that a deal is a deal— a promise is a promise?"

Peg only smiled. For she knew from experience that Lou was thinking out loud. She knew he would continue. And Lou did continue. "Decent people try to live up to their promises to other persons. Isn't that true? A person does try to live up to his promises to others."

Peg smiled and said nothing.

"But what about the promises to themselves? And what about all the New Year's resolutions that were made only a couple of months ago? Just think what wonderful things would have been achieved by people who made promises to themselves if they had lived up to those promises as diligently as they live up to their promises to others.

"And yet aren't promises to one's self just as important? Aren't they even more important than promises made to others? Shouldn't one try to live up to them just as diligently?

"And I've been thinking: Isn't it true that the difference between a successful person and mediocrity or failure is in proportion to that person's efforts to live up to the promises he makes to himself?

"I doubt if Helen would have had that heart attack had she lived up to her previous New Year's resolution to diet intelligently. We know she went to the doctor and he gave her a scientific diet. But after a few months she seemed to eat more than ever before.

"And Joe's family wouldn't be on relief. Joe wouldn't be sleeping in the gutters—if he had lived up to his New Year's resolution to stop drinking entirely.

"And how about Howard Smith? Howard wouldn't have been kicked out of Princeton if he had done his homework every day, just as he promised himself that he would last New Year's Eve at our party here."

Peg smiled.

"And, Peg, I made a promise too. And I just discovered what's really important to me is that I keep that promise to myself."

Peg stopped smiling, for she saw that Lou was serious. Very serious. And she listened intently as he continued: "Peg, last New Year's Eve I made a solemn vow to myself. And I promised God that every day of the new year I would try to show my appreciation for the blessings He has given me: *you and Kent.*

"I promised to make you happy in those little things in which I have been lax."

Lou looked directly into Peg's eyes as he said, "Peg, you can count on me to be home in time for dinner in the future. And you know I do keep my promises to others. From now on I shall also live up to the promises I make to myself. Should an emergency arise, I shall at least telephone you in plenty of time. You won't need to worry. And I know the reason you do worry is because you love me so."

Peg smiled again. But she stopped listening. She came over and put her arms around Lou and kissed him. And then she confided: "I made a New Year's promise to myself too, I promised that the next time you came home late without notifying me, I wouldn't make your life miserable as I have in the past. It was difficult, but tonight I did live up to my promise. And, Lou, I did find that it pays to keep one's promises to one's self."

"And they lived happily ever after."

5
COURAGE UNLIMITED

Courage grows from the heart.
–John Dryden

He came back from the shadows
of death and inspired millions with hope.

HOGAN

by OG MANDINO

They played the U.S. Open back in June, 1965, without the greatest professional golfer that ever lived. Ben Hogan, when told that he and all previous Open winners except the last five had to qualify for the "opportunity" to play in this year's Open, decided to sit this one out and watch television make heroes out of golfers that included many who never saw the day they could carry his golf clubs.

At the Colonial Open, a few months ago, Ben Hogan was presented with a trophy inscribed to "The Greatest Professional Golfer in History." As Ben accepted this award I wonder if the memory of a morning sixteen years ago flashed briefly across his mind.

Ben had just lost a play-off to Jimmy Demaret at Phoenix after winning the Bing Crosby Invitational and the Long Beach Open. He was tired and his thirty-seven-year-old legs were weary from the constant high pressure of tournament competition. He and his wife Valerie decided to pass up the next tournament at Tucson, and they headed for Fort Worth and home.

It was an early February morning in 1949. Patches of dark fog rolled like tumbleweed across prairie Highway 80. Ben's automobile headlights cut an abbreviated path through the mist. He drove slowly along the right shoulder of the road as he and Valerie, relaxing for the first time in months, chatted and planned their vacation. When Ben saw the oncoming headlights of a giant six-wheeler truck he inched closer to the culvert on his right. Suddenly two more headlights appeared in the fog. They lined up with the first pair to fill the narrow road as a Greyhound bus attempted to pass the six-wheeler. There was no room for the Hogan car.

Ben instinctively threw his body across Valerie a fraction of a second before the car and bus collided with a sickening crunch. The impact slammed the car engine back into the passenger compartment and the steering wheel was driven through the driver's seat. Ben's effort to save Valerie had prevented his own instant death.

When his broken body was removed from the wreckage it lay at the side of the road for nearly two hours because no one remembered to call an ambulance. Valerie, saved from serious injury by her husband's heroic action, watched helplessly as the little champion's color continued to fade. After the ambulance finally arrived there was a tortuous drive of 120 miles to the Hotel Dieu Hospital in El Paso. Ben had a fractured pelvis, a fractured shoulder, fractured ribs and a shattered ankle. Worst of all he was suffering from severe shock.

For thirty days Ben lay immobile, his body encased in plaster from chest to toes. Then he met a tougher competitor for his life. A blood clot formed in his leg and began its journey toward his heart. Ben's desperate friends placed the dying man on an Air Force bomber and flew him to New Orleans. He was nearly dead when the famed surgeon, Dr. Ochsner, operated and tied off the vena cava, a large vein which funnels blood into the right auricle of the heart. Sports editors throughout the country began passing out assignments to prepare Ben Hogan's obituary while they awaited word from the hospital. They waited in vain.

A week after the operation, letters began arriving for Ben from every corner of the world . . . each with the same message. The sender was praying for Ben's recovery. As Ben said later, "I had never experienced anything like that and I guess it was because I never played up to the crowds. I had always concentrated so hard on making every shot that I never allowed myself to pay attention to the gallery. Now they were writing by the thousands and it was a humbling experience to know that so many strangers really cared what happened to me."

Within a month Ben was home and beginning the slow

process of learning how to walk again. He weighed 96 pounds. That he would never play golf again was a foregone conclusion—except to Ben.

One morning, with sheer will power, he took his first step. He stumbled. He tried again and soon he was walking back and forth across the bedroom. Then he moved into the living room and began to complete lap after lap around the furniture while Valerie watched with pride and tearful admiration. Soon he began squeezing rubber balls to rebuild his arms and wrists.

One day he asked Valerie to bring him a golf club and using it as a cane he announced that he was going to walk around the block. The walks often seemed endless to Valerie, but Ben had developed his own system. He would walk as far as he could and then stop to rest. Each day he went farther and farther until finally he could circle the block nonstop. He was using the same system that had made him a champion: practice, concentration, practice, concentration. Because of his rearranged blood system his muscles continued to cramp and tire on him but he refused to quit. He tried swinging a club but the fractured shoulder and pelvis were taking long months to heal and his swing looked like that of a first-time-out duffer.

One morning in early fall an excited murmur raced through the Colonial Country Club. Members and club employees alike all stopped what they were doing and watched with fascination. Ben Hogan was on the putting green! Soon he began to walk with friends for a hole or two. In December he went out on the course and began playing . . . first one hole, then two, but the circulation still refused to function properly and his legs continued to swell. He carried a portable chair along and rested between shots. One day he tried playing an entire round. He paid for that by spending the next two days in bed.

In January, 1950, less than a year after his accident, Ben confounded every sportswriter in the country by entering the Los Angeles Open. Those in the know were betting that his legs would never carry him through the torturous 72 holes.

When he teed off for the first round, he had played less than eighty holes of golf since his accident. He came in with a 73! Next day he shot a 69! He followed that with another 69, and the same sportswriters who had written Ben off now began filling columns about the "comeback of the century." On the final day he tacked another 69 to his score, but Sammy Snead turned in one of the most sensational final rounds in the history of tournament golf and tied Ben with a 280 total for the 72 holes.

The following day Sam beat an exhausted Hogan in the play-off, but Ben was not disappointed. He had proven to himself that he was still a pro. He had also become a symbol for people with handicaps throughout the world, and another deluge of letters arrived at the Hogan residence. Now he was convinced that there was only one way to truly give these people the boost in morale they all sought. He had to win a major tournament. He set his sights on the U.S. Open in June.

The weather was hot and humid when the Open got under way at the Merion Country Club in Ardmore, Pennsylvania, on June 8. Sammy Snead was the favorite but the largest gallery followed Hogan. He shot a 72 on opening day which placed him eight strokes behind a young pro from Alabama who fired off a 64.

On Friday, Ben's putts began to drop and he limped in with a 69 to move within two strokes of the leader, Dutch Harrison. But Ben was already beginning to pay a horrible price in bodily torture. On the way back to the hotel with Valerie and his attorney, he had the car stopped while he fought off nausea and dizziness. Back in their hotel room Valerie helped him unwrap yards of rubber bandages from his swollen legs and then gently half-carried him to a warm bath where Ben sat for hours to ease the tightened muscles.

On Saturday he faced the toughest playing day of his career. Every nerve in his body seemed to be on fire while his legs, still swollen, had to carry him eight miles over 36 holes of pressure golf, 18 in the morning and another 18 in the afternoon. The temperature was in the mid-nineties and Ben was already drawing on that special reservoir that all champions have—guts.

He played the morning round in 72 and, since he always played against the course, not the individual players, he figured another 72 in the afternoon would give him the championship.

When he teed off for the final round, the huge gallery could see the obvious pain in the little man's face but it never showed in his swing. Perfected by thousands of hours of practice and hardened by ten years of professional competition, the precision that prompted one writer to compare Ben's swing to "a machine stamping out bottle caps" was still evident.

Ben made one concession to his disabilities. He had his caddy pick the ball out of the cup after he holed out on each hole to save him from bending his knees. He clicked off the first nine in the afternoon in 36 but, after he teed off on the tenth hole, a knifelike spasm shot through his left leg. Momentarily he was unable to walk and by the time he had completed the thirteenth hole he had decided to quit. The pain was unbearable. He could not move his leg. But as he tottered off the green toward an official he remembered all the letters he had received. How many people would he disappoint? How many would quit in their own personal struggle to overcome a handicap if their idol, Ben Hogan, quit?

He stumbled toward the fourteenth tee. His body was drenched in perspiration, some from the weather, more from the pain.

He lost a stroke to par on the fifteenth hole and another on the seventeenth. Just before teeing off on the last hole an official told him that he needed a par four to tie for the championship. A pained smile flickered across Ben's face. If he parred this hole he'd have to come out here tomorrow and play eighteen more holes of torture against two of the best golfers in the business, Lloyd Mangrum and George Fazio.

His drive cut the heart of the fairway and, as he approached his second shot he could already hear the standing ovation from the crowd surrounding the eighteenth green. Now his left leg was almost numb and there was a dull pain around his pelvic area. Common sense kept telling him to miss a shot and end the nightmare. He couldn't conceive playing another eighteen holes tomorrow; still his second shot was perfectly placed on the green and he was down in two putts to tie for the championship. The habit of always trying to do his best, no matter what the odds, had been too strong.

That night Ben slept the sleep of exhaustion but he arose refreshed and the swelling in his legs had almost disappeared. He played that day like the Hogan of old, shot a 69, and won the Open title by four strokes.

Ben won many more titles after that, but the indomitable courage of the little champion has placed those five rounds of golf high on the list of all-time athletic achievements. It was a triumph of mind and heart over physical adversity. It was an inspiration to millions who, day by day, struggle to overcome their own physical infirmities. It's a story that needed retelling because a new generation has already reached adulthood since Ben Hogan had his personal rendezvous with destiny on Highway 80.

But they wouldn't let Ben play in the Open. They thought he should "qualify." In my book he qualified a long time ago.

He left his legs in a foxhole but he still considers himself . . .

THE LUCKIEST MAN ALIVE

by RAYMOND A. TETZLAFF

Cheers of encouragement echoed through the halls of Percy Jones Hospital as war amputee Paul Kephart took his first cautious steps on his new artificial legs. He grinned right along with his appreciative audience of nurses, doctors and ward buddies as they watched him solo awkwardly on the limbs that would soon carry him back to a life of activity—and home.

"It was September, 1944, in Brest, France, when I lost my legs," Kephard reminisces. "The German shells were coming fast, shrieking and whining all around me. I plunged into a foxhole, but my legs stuck out. The next shell got them—quick and simple as that."

Paul literally got back on his feet at the hospital. He tells of endless hours of practicing: climbing stairs, walking in crowds, in and out of cars, up and down all manner of inclines. "I had to learn to walk all over again," he said. "But during the many months of uncertainty, anxiety and operations, those wonderful people at the hospital never let me give in to discouragement. Slowly, I began to realize that I had been given just one life to live, and that the way I was meant to do it was *standing up.*"

Kephard now lives in a ranch-style house in Beloit, Wisconsin, with his wife and two pretty young daughters who like nothing better than to join their Dad in a variety of sports. "He's a good dancer, too," they add whenever they speak of his many accomplishments.

As a salesman for National Biscuit Company, he drives a car and walks, climbs and carries with the best of them. A recent incident reveals just how much of a workout he gives his stand-in legs. "I returned them to a manufacturer not long ago," he said, "because the rivets and bolts had pulled loose. They wanted to know why my legs showed such unusual wear. It gave me a good feeling to be able to confess that they got beaten up from bowling, golfing, kicking a football, playing basketball and even climbing up a ladder to fix my roof. Could be, I'm a little too rough on them."

Paul is president of the Elks Club bowling league. His average is 160, but he keeps aiming for the record he set for himself when he rolled a high of 256.

Doctors often ask Kephart to visit other amputees. It gives them encouragement to know a man who makes a good life for himself and his family, even though both legs are gone. "I usually try to leave such people with the thought that ruling out self-pity is the first step to rehabilitation," he says thoughtfully, doubtless recalling his own long struggle.

In 1947, Paul had an opportunity to prove that the roots of courage grow deep and strong within those who have found compensation for their handicaps. He was one of a party on a moonlight boat ride when another boat came hurtling out of the shadows to split his craft in two. Eleven people were thrown into the water. Kephart clung to the airhorns of the floating prow and managed to pull two struggling women to the safety of his bit of wreckage. Then, with one arm supporting them, he used the other to gather a frightened eight-year-old girl into his group to await rescue.

Kephart's remarkable ability to function bravely and effectively under such tragic circumstances caused Congresswoman Edith N. Rogers to report his feat to the government. It was made a part of the Congressional Record.

Paul Kephart's grin widens as he flips a deprecatory hand over all this. "Don't call me hero," he protests. "I'm just the luckiest man alive. I have everything—my family, home and friends. And best of all, I know that I can help others learn how to live. Sometimes I wonder just how grateful I can get!"

*Paralyzed in a car crash, a promising
young artist gained faith and fulfilled
his destiny.*

PORTRAIT OF COURAGE

by THEODORE VRETTOS

On a warm August day in 1951, a car carrying five boys sped wildly over a winding road on the outskirts of Exeter, New Hampshire. It was several minutes past one o'clock and the boys were anxious to return to their summer jobs in an apple orchard nearby.

Glen Fowler sat apprehensively in the rear seat while the car careened noisily around the sharp corners. Suddenly and without warning, the car came to a hairpin curve which the driver was unable to negotiate. . . .

In a matter of moments an ambulance hurried to the scene—four of the boys were rushed to Exeter's hospital. The fifth, Glen Fowler, was left in the wrecked car, presumably dead.

For two hours, Glen remained there unconscious. Then the ambulance finally came back for him, the doctors felt his pulse and discovered a faint beat. Quickly, they rushed Glen to the same hospital. But when the team of surgeons waiting there to operate on the boy saw him they shook their heads. The youth's neck was broken in three places, and he appeared to be paralyzed from head to foot.

They treated him for shock, wrapped him warmly in blankets, and rushed him under police escort to the Deaconess Hospital in Boston. There, the boy was subjected to an exhausting series of examinations. Hundreds of reflex tests could prove only one thing: Glen Fowler, at the age of seventeen, had been changed into a useless quadriplegic. A large nerve at the base of his neck leading from the central nervous system was severed beyond repair. This prevented any brain messages from reaching his four limbs.

Glen remained on his back for five painful months, strapped with weights and splints. With most of his body already dead, he prayed that the rest of him would not live. Gradually, he began to mistrust both himself and God and withdrew completely from all contacts with the outside world.

Alarmed over his weakening condition, the doctors at Deaconess decided to transfer Glen to the Massachusetts Hospital School in Canton. Here, he was placed under a strenuous program of occupational and physiotherapy. But he showed no desire to help himself, and his condition grew worse.

One day an attractive nurse named Joanne Rogers walked into his room. "Hello, grouch!" she said cheerfully.

He did not reply. When he looked into her smiling face and saw how her eyes danced to an inner vitality, it made him bitterly resentful.

"Are you going to stay in that bed the rest of your life?" Joanne teased. When again he did not answer, she stepped out of his room momentarily and came back with a wheelchair. "Come," she said, "you and I are taking a spin together."

But Glen wanted no part of that wheelchair. He closed his eyes and tried to slump back into his bed until she left the room. However, Joanne did not give up. She came back the next day— and the next. Each time, she placed the wheelchair at the base of Glen's bed. Finally, on an impulse to please her, he agreed to try it. While Joanne held him firmly under the armpits, he managed to slide from the edge of his bed into the wheelchair. It was a long and tedious task, but Joanne did not seem to mind. Time ticked off a year while she cajoled, scolded and encouraged him. Slowly, he began to like the chair—grudgingly at first, then with a warming sense of looking forward to the routine.

Now the first step was over. The desire to live had been resurrected within his heart, but there still remained a more difficult obstacle to be overcome: a lack of interest in any occupation.

While in high school, Glen had shown a remarkable aptitude for art. He had won several awards and his work was rapidly being recognized in North Shore art circles at the time of the accident. But that was all part of the past, Glen reminded himself as he closed his mind to his dreams of becoming a great painter. In his despair he rejected an unjust God who first gave him a talent and then took it away.

One day, deep in the throes of melancholy, he suddenly experienced an overwhelming urge to express his feelings in the one way he knew—on canvas. He asked one of the doctors for a brush and paints.

When the materials were brought into his room and placed on his bed the air seemed charged with tension. The doctor helped Glen into his wheelchair and watched silently as the young patient strained to pick up one of the brushes. Every muscle in his warped body tugged and pulled in an effort to grip the brush in his finger—but it was hopeless.

The doctor moved close to Glen. He took the brush and held it before his eyes and, with no trace of pity in his voice, said, "Glen, this isn't as bad as it seems to you at the moment. I realize that you have no strength in your arms—but from your neck up, you are strong."

"Do you expect me to paint with my neck?" Glen asked rebelliously.

"With your teeth, Glen, your *teeth!*" the doctor said.

Glen tried to laugh, but even this pained him. "You've had your fun for today, Doc," he snapped, "Now go away and leave me alone!"

The doctor persisted. "Glen, this is not a joke—believe me. There is no difference between controlling a brush with your fingers and doing the same thing with your teeth. In fact, you can get a firmer grip with your teeth."

"So you want me to paint with my teeth?" Glen's attempt at a laugh was bitter.

"Glen, do you think that God's gift to you is limited to your fingers?" the doctor asked as he touched him gently on the arm. "An artist is great, not in his fingers, but in his *heart and soul.*"

The doctor left the room then, and his words began to burn their way into Glen's mind. When he was certain that he was alone, he bent toward the bed and seized one of the brushes in his teeth. Moving his head awkwardly, he dipped it into a small container of red paint and with slow, painful strokes began to paint. There was something desperate and frightening in the wild dashes of red—but the work was his own, *his very own!*

Taking a deep breath, he reached for another brush and a fresh piece of paper. This time he was careful and patient. He worked with deliberation and determination, even stopping several times to clean his brushes. Finally, he leaned back exhausted but happy, and viewed his first painting. It was crude and uneven, but it vibrated with meaning—a quiet pastoral scene with mountains and a stream and colorful trees lay before him.

Glen was now ready to go home. After five years in the hospital, his first concern was how to pay off the enormous bills from the hospital and the doctors. His father's salary at the Navy Yard was scarcely adequate to feed and clothe a wife and four younger children, let alone cope with $10,000 in medical expenses.

Fortunately, accident insurance would cover almost half of the bill, but that still left more than $5,000 to cast its shadows on Glen's already overburdened mind. On an impulse, he decided to enroll at the Famous Artists School in Westport, Connecticut. After submitting a few of his drawings, he was granted a full three-year scholarship, and *hope* opened its compassionate arms to welcome him.

Glen held his first exhibition before he had completed his work at the art school. When the show closed, he had sold over twenty paintings for a total of $1,200.

This was but a starter for other sales to follow. Within a matter of months, 150 of his paintings had been purchased. He was soon able to meet not only his own medical bills but also to free his family from debt.

Many honors and awards have come to this young man since then. And not the least of these is a charming wife—the devoted Joanne Rogers who first encouraged him to return to life in a hospital ward. They were married in Glen's family home in Newburyport in 1958, then moved to Beverly, Massachusetts, where Joanne works the three-to-seven shift at the local hospital.

"I am a happy man," Glen says. "Not only am I fulfilling the work that I was meant to do, but I have regained my faith in God and in myself."

6

MIND UNLIMITED

It is the mind that maketh good or ill, that maketh wretch or happy, rich or poor.
—Edmund Spenser

Here's the secret of preparing your
mind to achieve any goal you set
for yourself.

THE SUREST WAY IN THE WORLD TO ATTRACT SUCCESS—OR FAILURE

by HAROLD SHERMAN

"You might know this would happen to me!"

Is this a comment you have made, not once, but many times, when things have gone wrong? It's human nature to feel, when something unhappy has happened, that it may happen again. Your fear of it may cause you to picture the possibility of its recurrence and, without realizing it, you have set forces in motion to attract similar conditions to you. Then, when face to face with another unpleasant experience, you testify to the fact that you have anticipated it, have even helped create it by saying, "You might know this would happen to me!"

Certainly—you *knew* it was going to happen—and it did. Your faith in "things going wrong" caused the "power of TNT" within you to work *against* you instead of *for* you.

There is a great law of mind by which your thinking and your conduct should always be guided: "Like attracts like."

Think good thoughts; you will eventually attract good things. Think bad thoughts, you will ultimately attract bad things.

Simple—easy to remember—but also easy to forget. Even though you know the consequences of harboring destructive, apprehensive emotions—when fear and worry assail you—don't you often permit them to exist within your consciousness? We all do.

That's why our prayers for deliverance from a difficult or distressing situation are not answered.

You must *prepare* your mind to *receive* that for which you are asking before you can attract it to you—before the God Power within can help bring it to you?

How is this done? By giving the God Power the right mental pictures to work with—reinforced by your faith in God as well as in yourself.

Check back now on some of your prayers that were not answered. How did you *feel* at the time—what were your *thoughts?* Did you *picture* clearly and calmly and confidently, in your mind's eye, what you wanted the God Power to help attract to you? Or through fear did you keep on picturing the trouble you were in? If you did, then these very pictures only intensified your trouble, made it more a part of you.

Every time your "voice of fear" talks to you while you are praying, pouring such hopeless, negative thoughts into your consciousness as: "Prayer won't do any good; you can't get out of this fix; it's going to be worse tomorrow," you can be sure that your troubles will not be relieved.

There is a great truth in the old, old saying: "God helps those who help themselves."

The surest way in the world to attract trouble is to *picture* the possibility of more trouble coming to you!

This isn't helping yourself or helping the God Power to help you. When an architect draws a blueprint of a house, if he makes some mistakes in calculation or design, they will show up in the finished building because the builder will faithfully and unquestioningly follow the blueprint. The architect is supposed to know his business. If the construction turns out to be wrong or weak, the architect is the one who must bear the responsibility.

You are supposed to know what you want in life. If your feelings get mixed up, through fear or worry, if you are indecisive, lacking in confidence or faith, judgment or experience, you won't be able to picture yourself *doing* or *being* or *having* the right things in your future and, as a consequence, your "power of TNT" within will be given the wrong blueprints to work on.

Get this point clearly in mind: You supply the material (by the nature of your thoughts) out of which your creative power builds your future. If the material is inferior, comprised of mental pictures of failure, despair, defeat and the like, you can readily see that only unhappy results can be materialized from them.

If you are anticipating the worst while hoping for the best, you will get the worst. The things that happen to you are in direct accordance with the things wherein you place your faith. Believe you are licked—and you are. Your belief instructs the Power Within to produce failure.

Trouble is the product of wrong thinking. Straighten out your thinking and your troubles must vanish. They cannot continue to exist because they have been created and kept alive by wrong thinking—and a change of mental attitude always brings about a change of conditions and experiences.

You cannot think love and hate at the same time—either one or the other must dominate. So it is with every constructive or destructive feeling. There is a continuous battle going on in our consciousness for the ascendancy of good and bad feelings. As creatures of free will and free choice, it is up to us to develop and maintain emotional control. It is our job to conquer our fears and worries, our likes and dislikes, and to direct our desires into right channels. Once we do this, we begin to get right results in every department of our lives; things commence to happen as they should happen; success becomes a regular pattern, in place of failure.

The admonition: "Don't trouble trouble 'til trouble troubles you," is a good one. Because you have had an unfortunate experience is no indication that this experience need be repeated in your future—unless you start brooding about it, fearing its repetition, even inviting it by a continued picture of a like occurrence.

Your feelings are dynamite. They have the power to make or break you. Take inventory of your feelings this very minute—about others, about your problems, your future. Are you worried, apprehensive, resentful, fearful, when you should be relaxed, self-confident, in good spirits, filled with courage and faith?

Whatever conditions you are facing at the moment are the result of your past thinking—good and bad. These conditions cannot change until you have first changed your thinking.

Do you wish to attract more trouble? You can easily do it!

Just persist in maintaining a wrong mental attitude toward someone or some experience. That's all you need to do, and you'll see how quickly and positively this power within will serve you—in reverse.

Remember—you are the architect and this "power of TNT" is the builder. It operates like a magnet, attracting to you what you picture.

Things first happen in your mind before they can happen in this outer world. What are you picturing? Do you want it to happen? If not, you are the only one who can prevent it. Your future success or failure is in your hands—where it should be.

Don't ever say again: "You might know this would happen to me!" Say instead: "I know only Good is going to happen to me—because my thinking is right."

The greatest and most intricate electronic
computer ever built will never approach
the capability of your mind.

YOUR SOURCE OF POWER

by NAPOLEON HILL

Of all the great men I have known, Thomas A. Edison intrigued me most. Perhaps this was due to the fact that despite his lack of formal education, he became the foremost man of achievement in the field of the sciences.

I was intrigued also because of the mental attitude in which Mr. Edison related himself to his affliction of deafness. When I asked him if he had not found his work very difficult because of his deafness, he replied: "To the contrary, deafness has been a great help to me. It has saved me from having to listen to a lot of worthless chatter from men who did not know what they were talking about, and it has taught me to *hear from within.*"

The latter part of that statement is very significant, especially to the person who is seeking the way to peace of mind through understanding of self. By transmuting his affliction into a positive mental attitude, Mr. Edison learned how to tune in on Infinite Intelligence and get his knowledge from an infallible source.

Thomas A. Edison was far and away the calmest man I have ever known. He had no frustration complexes. He had no fears. He had no regrets about anything or anyone. He had no grandiose ideas of his own importance, but he did have humility of the heart, which made him truly great.

His understanding of the benefits of closing the door behind disappointing experiences was profoundly reflected in the fact that before he perfected the incandescent electric light, he met with more than ten thousand separate and distinct failures.

Think of a mind which is capable of setting a goal, and then letting nothing turn it aside until that goal is reached, and you have a perfect picture of the quality which made Mr. Edison great.

Once I asked Mr. Edison, "What would you have done if you had not finally uncovered the secret of the incandescent electric lamp?"

With a merry twinkle in his eyes he replied: "I would be in my laboratory working now, instead of wasting my time talking with you."

Mr. Edison knew no such reality as "failure" because he had discovered the supreme secret which leads to peace of mind and understanding of the source and power of the mind. Without the aid of that supreme secret, Mr. Edison never would have become the world's number one inventor.

Because of his knowledge of the supreme secret, Thomas A. Edison carried on through more than ten thousand definite failures in his search for the solution of a problem. I wonder how many people know the number of failures the average man can survive without quitting and giving up the ghost in despair. To satisfy my curiosity on this subject I once made a survey through which I examined men and women to ascertain their staying qualities in the face of failure or defeat.

The majority of them quit trying when overtaken one time by defeat. A very small percentage of them kept on trying a second time. But by far the greater number quit even before meeting with defeat because they expected it and quit before they really started.

Needless to suggest, there were no Edisons and no Fords in this group.

They were the average run-of-the-mill of humanity who somehow never got around to recognizing the master key to riches with which they were endowed at birth: a master key consisting of their ability to tune in and appropriate the power of Infinite Intelligence by the simple process of conditioning their minds to receive and use this great universal power.

I have observed two important facts concerning men who are successful in their chosen occupations and those who are not. The successes speak in the future tense of yet unattained objectives which they intend to achieve. The failures speak in the past tense, of their defeats and their disappointments. I have never known the rule to fail.

I have observed another trait concerning successes and failures. The successful man usually speaks in complimentary terms of other men who are succeeding, while the failure usually has a word of criticism of the men who are succeeding.

Envy and revenge are very ugly words. More ugly still is the character of the person who indulges in these emotions. They represent emotions against which the doors of one's mind must be tightly closed if one is to enjoy peace of mind.

The source of Mahatma Gandhi's influence over more than a hundred million of his followers was a great mystery to many people. They could not understand how a man who had no money, no military equipment, no organized soldiers could defy the powerful British Government and so successfully get away with it.

What was the source of Gandhi's power? He simply mobilized the mind-power of more than a hundred million people, who fixed their minds upon the major objective of routing the British and freeing India. Time turned this purpose into action which forced the British to withdraw. *Remember, organized mind-power is greater than organized military power.*

Note, however, this important feature of the Gandhi mind-power. He freed his mind of all desire for revenge, all hatred, all desire for personal aggrandizement. He sought no robes of honor for himself; nor did he seek any form of material riches. All he sought was the privilege of mobilizing the mind-power of the Indian people for the purpose of gaining their freedom from British rule.

There is something profound about the powers of a man who moves under this type of impersonal motive. There is something truly great about the man who seeks freedom and benefits for others, while he seeks nothing for himself but the privilege of serving. Perhaps his "something," whatever it is, was responsible for the success of George Washington's armies when they were fighting against great odds, for the independence of this nation.

Close the doors of your mind to everything which caused

you anxiety, fear, envy, greed and the desire of something for nothing. The penalty for failure to close the doors will be loss of the peace of mind which you are seeking.

Through no fault of your own, you lost your job. There are two moves you can make. First, you can nurse your wounded feeling until they fester into resentment and hatred of your former employer. In that frame of mind you will find it extremely difficult to get another job, no matter how skilled in your occupation you may be. No employer wants a person with a negative mind around any place of business. He has a bad effect on the customers and other employees.

Secondly, you can transmute your temporary frustration into a determined will to get a better job than the one you lost, close the door on your old job and start right where you stand to find just the job you desire. If you speak of your former employer at all, be sure to speak of him in complimentary terms. That may not help him any, but it will do *you* a lot of good.

You have been injured, perhaps unjustly, by someone who works with you in your occupation. Here you are face to face with an opportunity to learn whether or not you have within you the makings of bigness. If you are potentially a great person, you will forgive and close the door behind you on the incident.

If you have not the foundation for greatness, you will find ways and means of striking back at the person who injured you, and possibly go so far as to cause that person to lose his job. In that event you will be the more unfortunate person of the two, for truly any person who expresses any form of revenge is unfortunate. Revenge is like a boomerang. It often comes back to wound the person who sets it into motion against another.

You have held your present position for a long while without getting the promotions to which you believe you are entitled. There are two things you can do about it. First, you can open wide the doors to your mind so that Old Man Grudge can enter and make you grouchy. In that event, you may never get the promotions you desire, but you will be almost sure to "get the gate" sooner or later.

Secondly, you can start right where you stand and apply the habit of going the extra mile by rendering more service and better service than you are now being paid for, and doing it in a pleasing mental attitude. By this method, and this method alone, you can make yourself so valuable that your employer cannot afford to keep you in your present job, but he will voluntarily move you up into another station. If he is so lacking in imagination as not to recognize your better type of service, then someone else may recognize it and your reward may come from an entirely different source.

When it comes to the entertainment of anger or hurt feelings, remember they, also, are to be put behind that closed door. It is most important for you to know that no one may make you angry or hurt your feelings in any manner whatsoever, *without your willing cooperation.*

Your state of mind is something you can control completely. And you may be surprised to learn, after you become better acquainted with this "door closing" idea, how easily you can take possession of your mind and condition it for the attainment of any purpose you desire.

No one can control the actions of others, or many of the circumstances of life which tend to make one angry, *but anyone may control his reactions to these actions and circumstances.* Your mind is your own. You are the sole supervisor of its reactions to every circumstance which affects your life. Learn to close the door of your mind and shut out the negative reactions if you wish to find peace of mind and lasting prosperity.

He frightened the stagehands when he called for . . .

THE "BIG ME"

by MARJORIE SPILLER NEAGLE

The story is told that on opening night, before the great Enrico Caruso became famous, he was overcome by stage fright. As he stood in the wings, his throat contracted with a spasm of terror. Sweat poured from him. He was on the verge of running away.

Suddenly a thought struck him.

"The little me on the outside is strangling the big me on the inside. The me that wants to sing . . . that *can* sing . . . must come out."

He began a whispered shout. "Get out of the way! Get out! Get out!"

The stagehands looked at him frightened and other members of the cast wondered if Caruso had taken leave of his senses.

By the time the cue came for the singer to make his entrance, the "little me" had been routed and the "big me" was in command.

After Caruso finished his aria the audience rose to its feet, cheering and shouting, "Bravo!"

A powerful force had been put into the person of Caruso. Only when he recognized that a weak force was holding it back and acted upon that knowledge, did the stronger one come through.

7

HEALTH UNLIMITED

*He who has health has hope; and he
who has hope, has everything.*
—Arabian Proverb

If tension and worry are weapons
you are using to commit slow suicide,
this advice is for you.

HOW TO LIVE LONGER

by FRANK ROSE

"The most common cause of death today is suicide." This startling statement was made to me recently by a doctor friend while I was interviewing him for a health magazine.

"But, Doc," I protested, "the suicide rate isn't that high. I have some figures on it right here." I started groping through my briefcase. He waved his hand impatiently.

"I know the statistics. I'm not talking about official suicide with guns and other lethal instruments. Most people choose a slower method. But it's just as fatal in the long run. I'm talking about worry, pessimism and fear. They're the greatest killers of our time!"

After this revealing interview, I spent several weeks researching the subject. I read dozens of books, pamphlets and magazine articles. I talked with a score of physicians, psychologists and clergymen. All agreed that the hectic tempo of modern living with its resultant tension is a serious national problem. All voiced the opinion that millions of Americans are slowly killing themselves with the deadly weapon of anxiety.

As one doctor put it, "Ailments caused by negative thinking account for more sickness than all other diseases combined. Such sickness is not imaginary, as many suppose. It is just as real as a broken leg and usually far more serious."

"What is the answer?" I asked.

He shrugged his shoulders. "Get people to stop worrying. Get them to relax. But don't ask me how. I don't know." He stared out of the office window for several moments with a troubled expression on his face. "Nowadays," he continued, "people always seem to be expecting the worst and that's what they usually get. They fail to realize that most of their afflictions are self-created, that negative thoughts always produce negative results. They've lost their confidence—or faith, or whatever you want to call it—that things will go well and this vital lack is short-circuiting their health and their ability to cope adequately with life's problems."

A clergyman expanded this point. "Faith is the answer, all right, but not the vague, passive attitude that usually passes by that name. Real faith is not hope or desire; it is the optimism that comes from inside. It is, above all, a creative force. It makes good things happen.

"Too many people today associate faith with purely religious activities. They don't bring its dynamic power into their workaday lives and, without it, they are ill equipped to ward off the swarms of troubles that beset us all these days. Worry stems from fear, and fear is an outright admission of lack of faith. A round-the-clock working faith is the only armor against worry and fear."

All of the persons interviewed agreed that a working faith of some kind was the solution to our growing health problem, and that the public needs to be educated to the fact that our health and happiness depend upon our mental attitude.

But how can our thoughts make us sick? To many people this is incomprehensible. They think of their minds and emotions as something apart and totally different from their bodies. This is not true, as research and discoveries in the field of psychosomatic medicine have clearly proven. The mind and body are interrelated. What affects one affects the other.

William James, the noted psychologist, defined an emotion as "the state of mind that manifests itself by a perceptible change in the body." It is easy to verify the truth of this statement from your own experience. Remember the last time that you became angry? Were you affected only in your mind, or did your face flush, your eyes widen and your muscles tighten and tremble?

Think back to a time of fear. Do you recall the creeping sensation at the back of your neck, the lump in your throat, the tight knot in your stomach, your pounding heart? Have you ever fainted at the sight of blood? Or been sick to your stomach because of disgust? All of us are familiar with the splitting headache and varied pains that invariable accompany worry and tension.

None of these effects is imaginary. They are caused by the tightening of muscles and the squeezing of nerves and blood vessels in reaction to emotions. If such a state of mind is prolonged—and with many persons it is continual—it can lead to sickness as serious as any caused by germs.

Doctors warn us that becoming angry or upset can cause the coronary arteries of our heart to squeeze tightly. In time, this can produce a heart attack that is just as fatal as one brought on by physical causes. In fact, the former are much more common than the latter. Likewise, an ulcer resulting from anxiety is just as real and painful as one brought on by the wrong diet. These are just two examples of the many hundreds of illnesses which people bring upon themselves by their mental attitudes.

According to Dr. John A. Schindler, author and former Chief Physician of the Monroe Wisconsin Clinic, "The human body is heir to a thousand different ailments and one of them appears to be as common as all other 999 put together. It formerly was known as psychosomatic illness. And it is *not* a disease in which the patient merely *thinks* he is sick."

What is the solution to this mounting toll of misery and ill health? The American Medical Association tells us that we must learn to control our thoughts and to think right. It lists eight excellent rules for us to follow:

"1. Quit looking for a knock in your motor. 2. Learn to like your work. 3. Have at least one hobby. 4. Learn to like people. 5. Learn to be satisfied when you can't easily change your situation. 6. Learn to accept adversity. 7. School yourself to learn to say the cheerful, helpful and humorous thing. 8. Learn to face your challenge and your problems with confidence and decision."

This is helpful advice as far as it goes, but it overlooks the most important remedy of all: faith—faith that all will be well, faith that faith will make it so. A vast number of people today are facing life without the buoyant support of this dynamic force. Many of them have a kind of faith, all right, but it is something they keep hidden in a holy niche of their consciousness, taking it out for Sundays and special religious occasions and then putting it carefully away again. They seem to feel that faith belongs solely to the spiritual realm and has no connection with the material world of everyday living. They fail to weave its golden strands into the fabric of their daily life and thus are helpless to handle the constant difficulties they meet.

They worry about their health, finances, homes, jobs, taxes, old age, atomic warfare, the weather, their neighbors. Their minds throng with a thousand flitting images of half-formed worries, doubts and apprehensions. Nothing is too insignificant or farfetched for them to fret about. In fact, a good many persons spend most of their waking hours brooding about something or other. All of this unnecessary tension, this suicidal morbidity, adds up to just one thing: fear—fear of what the future will bring. And this in turn, boils down to the fact that faith is not operating in their lives as it should.

In order for anyone to acquire the faith that will keep him well, it is first necessary for him to realize that it is not a lot of mystical nonsense but is an established scientific fact. It is the heart and core of psychosomatic medicine. It is just as real as electricity.

You do not have to accept it on someone else's say-so; you can experience its truth and effectiveness in your own life any time you desire. Just shove worry and fear to one side and learn to relax. Take each day as it comes and do not fret about tomorrow. This does not mean that you should not plan for the future, but only that you should never worry about it. There is a big difference. Planning is healthy and constructive. It is the positive approach to life. Worry is unhealthy and destructive. It is the negative approach.

If there is the slightest doubt in your mind as to your present thinking habits, it will repay you to examine them carefully and honestly. You may discover that you have been killing yourself on the installment plan. If such be the case, do not worry. Just make up your mind to face the present with courage and the future with optimism and let faith handle the rest.

If you can't go to sleep when counting
sheep, here are some other suggestions
to help you woo Morpheus.

HOW ABOUT YOUR INSOMNIA?

by JACK MEYER

If someone in your vicinity says, "I slept like a baby last night,"
do you feel from the bottom of your insomnia like taking a poke
at him to erase that well-rested look from his face? Would you
also like to have it understood that there is grave doubt in your
mind that he is telling the truth?

Perhaps you suspect that you look similar to the bleary-eyed
gargoyle you thought you saw leering at your bedroom window
in the early-morning fog. What's more, you just can't find a
good excuse to kick around and blame your insomnia on. You
could kick something else, like the hassock or highboy, but that
would be painful and hence defeat your purpose.

Oh sure, you've had insomnia before. You never came right
out and gave it a name, because you hoped it wouldn't happen
again. Now that it is happening more and more often, you can't
avoid giving it its legitimate name.

Since insomniacs aren't an organized lot who elect officers,
conduct meetings or engage in campaigns, they can't come to
any sweeping conclusions to eliminate their problems. Anyone
on his own is bound to be victimized by those resourceful worry-
demons that heckle and harass you beyond the point of no
return—or so it seems. Once you relax, your guard is down and
you have to start coping with your sleeplessness. That is, unless
you are just too tired to stay awake at this point—a refreshing
alternative that automatically robs you of your insomniac
standing.

Sleep is a necessity recognized the world over. The average

American goes to bed in the evening. The time of evening varies according to occupation, social habits and whether you watch the late-late TV show. If you are of the rigid-routine rank, you possibly check the thermostat, lock the doors, put out the cat, brush your teeth and do any number of tedium-producing chores before bedding down on your inner-spring. Variations on this theme are many. But whatever the ritual, eventually we all fall into the same class—would-be sleepers.

Here is a familiar picture. Stretched out prone or supine or curled into a crescent, you punch your pillow, bunching it into the right shape or comfortable hollow. A few wriggles and squirms and you're off. That is, you *thought* you were off. That curtain flapping in the window is no dream, and "oh my aching back," how about shifting to the other side of the bed which has fewer rocks in the mattress?

A few adjustments later, you try again. Now you assume more fantastic positions, like the pretzel, the corkscrew, the sheepdog or the Hindu, all of which feel fine for a few minutes. How about that old trick of closing the eyes and grunting like a contented water buffalo?

"We must not take chances on postponing this matter. . . ." Whoops! How did that old speech get in here? Speculations, reviews, previews and just plain worthless niggling ideas keep building up. Problems and doubts are racing around in your fully awakened brain like greyhounds chasing a rabbit around a giant racetrack.

It could, and does, go on indefinitely. You give the pillow another sharp blow. Count sheep—that's it! Uncle Bill used to say that did the trick for him, but then he was a sheep rancher, and counting them must have given him a sense of security. Counting "one, two, three, four" is murderously dull and ought to put anyone to sleep. "one thousand one, one thousand two . . ." counting out loud, much louder than you thought, not only keeps *you* awake but wakes up the rest of the household as well.

When all is quiet and righteous indignation has simmered down, you say to yourself, "Nice try," and scrap sheep counting. Now the thought flashes onto a mystic screen, "Recite poetry." Some rhythmic lines float to the surface, but you can't get enough of them together to make sense. You haven't recited poetry since you were in the eighth grade. You sit up, swaying back and forth in tempo with "Tell me not in mournful numbers, Life is but an empty . . ." an empty *what!* You cudgel your brain and, by that time, sleep seems two million light-years away.

Worry is certainly a sleep robber, especially for those who are fingernail chewers or thumb-twiddlers to boot. If the worries stem from the weight of decisions that must be made in business or personal life, it would be best to face them as squarely as possible or consult a trustworthy person qualified to help you find the answer. One can't wish problems away, but you can lighten them by putting them in their proper prospective.

My doctor set me straight on several facts about insomnia. "It's quite common," he said, deflating me. "Everyone should evolve his own dependable system to resolve the problem." I mumbled something about trying to help, but the doctor seemed lost in thought. In fact, he looked sleepy. "There aren't any snap cures," he yawned.

This all sounds neat and pat in the doctor's office, but I bet him dominoes to dictionaries that it wouldn't last until I got within a foot of my bed that night. After considerable reading, probing and experimenting, I compiled ten points for my friend, the doctor, to sanction. He said, "It looks to me as if the sleeping-pill trade will decline when this gets out."

I hesitate labeling these *rules,* for the connotation has a tendency to rouse us into taking a firm stand to carry them out. This won't woo any sleep.

Assuming, then, that you have a place to sleep and that your rent is paid up, here are some ideas that do not call for undue cunning or wily tricks:

1. Bedtime should not be worry time or planning time for tomorrow. Mental activity of this kind is not conducive to relaxation.

2. Your bed should be comfortable, not too soft or too hard. Use subdued colors in the bedroom and, if possible, do not use the room for other activities such as sewing, desk work or watching TV.

3. Do not be overly concerned or fretful about getting your eight hours of sleep. People vary in their requirements and you may not need that much.

4. Almost everyone has a "getting-ready-for-bed" routine. These preparations, by their very monotony, bring on somnolence. If you must read in bed, better choose something fairly dull so that the drowsy atmosphere created does not dissipate.

5. Don't fret if you don't go to sleep right away. Quiet rest without loss of consciousness is beneficial, too. Shut out noises and light. This is particularly true of unusual sounds such as a dripping faucet, a flapping curtain or thumping blinds.

6. When hunger gnaws, don't resist that snack which will settle the demon. Crackers and milk may sound unexciting, but will fill that hollow which may have grown to proportions of the Grand Canyon while you were wasting your time fighting it.

7. Smoking and caffeinic drinks, especially if used excessively, may be too stimulating for some. Others, whose systems have adjusted to these stimulants, will snooze away unperturbed.

8. Certain positions are more restful than others. Lying on the side is recommended for adults with a pillow of the right thickness to alleviate shoulder or neck muscle strain. Don't get the idea, however, that if you go to sleep on your side you will wake up in the same position. It can happen, but you may just have ended up there after changing positions about forty times during the night.

9. Stretching and yawning help you to let down. Try a nightly "I don't care" attitude. In fact, sprawling and stretching and then reversing the stretch to what I call a "slumping-in-a-heap" feeling makes you feel like drifting off.

10. Your digestion, possible allergies, attitudes and general health play a part in your quest for rest. If you are an insomniac of long standing, losing night after night of sleep, you may not be a subject for self-help. Consult your physician for remedial treatment of possible underlying causes.

You can kid about insomnia just so far, then you've had it. If it is of any help to know that many famous people at one time or another belonged to the ranks of *insomniacs*, cherish the thought. As for me, I'm too slee-eepy!

Tears are the safety valve that could
help you add years to your life.

MEN, IT'S OKAY TO CRY!

by RALPH E. PROUTY

One of the most emotion-packed moments in sports history came on July 4, 1939, when the New York Yankees held a "Lou Gehrig Day" at Yankee Stadium. Seldom has there been such a spontaneous outpouring of feeling for an athlete. The recipient of it all, the "Iron Horse," had reached the end of the trail. Actually Gehrig was a dying man, though none of his teammates or fans suspected it.

As the compliments and praises were showered upon him by such dignitaries as Mayor Fiorello LaGuardia and Postmaster General James A. Farley, Lou gulped and fought back the tears. But when Manager Joe McCarthy presented him with a silver trophy from his Yankee teammates, the big athlete broke down and cried.

Other athletes have shed tears in public, and with less provocation. Not many baseball players would cry upon learning that they had been sold to the Yankees. One who did was a Cardinal outfielder, Enos Slaughter. After sixteen years with St. Louis, Slaughter was unexpectedly sold to the Yanks. Enos was so shocked at the idea that the Cards would let him go after such long and faithful service that his only outlet was in tears.

Basketball star Bob Cousy shed a few tears at a celebration in his honor at the Boston Garden. At thirty-four, Cousy was retiring after thirteen years with the Boston Celtics to start a coaching career. The accolade, including a telegram from President John F. Kennedy, was more than the cage star could take. His feeling overflowed through his eyes.

Athletes aren't the only grown men known to cry as an involuntary expression of emotion. Shortly after V-E Day, a colonel in the United States Army was driving through Germany in his small staff car. He passed lines of ragged, tired German soldiers, just released from prison camps, now trudging hundreds of miles back to their homes and families.

"Strange," said the colonel later, "last week I hated their guts. Now I suddenly saw them as human beings hurrying back home to become husbands, rear children and till the soil. Before I realized it, I found that I was crying."

Our culture has taught us for thousands of years that crying is unmanly. Only women weep. Men—especially strong men— suffer in silence. King Lear, Shakespeare's tragic hero, after being dispossessed by his two daughters, suffers the greatest heartbreak of his life. But will he weep? He will not. He says:

"Let not woman's weapons, water drops,
    Stain my man's cheeks!"

In other cultures it is quite permissible for man to shed tears in public. Among the Maoris of New Zealand it is as common and accepted a thing for the warriors to weep as it is for the women. Eskimo men also weep without losing status in the eyes of the community.

It is not uncommon in Latin countries to see men shed tears in public. Perhaps the French, Italians and Spanish are simply more emotional by nature than the rest of us. There is also the possibility that their men realize the value of a good cry now and then.

Scientists have been telling us for the past few years that crying may actually be good for us on occasion. In a recent address to the American Chemical Society, Dr. James O. Bond, distinguished epidemiologist, said that modern man might add years to his life if he would break down and weep once in a while or else find a male equivalent for tears.

"Weeping," said Dr. Bond, "has both a protective and a tonic effect—protective in that it guards the organism against the damaging effects of shock, tonic in that it serves to restore the organism to a state of stability."

When we undergo a severe emotional experience, tension builds up within the body. The body demands some way to release this tension. Crying is nature's way of providing that emotional release. When we refuse to shed tears, the whole body takes the brunt of the emotional discharge. This may upset delicate glandular balances, cause chemical changes in the body, raise hob with your nerves and actually make your body ill.

Noting that American men have been taught that "only sissies cry," Dr. Bond cites the case of the Eskimo man, who is free to weep without the finger of scorn being pointed at him. The doctor notes, at the same time, that psychosomatic disorders are practically unknown among Eskimo men.

Any connection? A good many scientists are beginning to think so. Dr. Walter Alvarez of the Mayo Clinic bears out what Dr. Bond has already said: "Deep emotion that has no vent in tears makes the other organs weep."

Special studies made by the United States Army indicate that men will resort to many reactions before they allow themselves to shed tears. They will grit their teeth, clench their fists, vomit, even faint. But, being red-blooded American boys, they won't cry. That's for softies.

Suppose you saw a picture of a man in public life—a man you respected highly—shedding tears. Would you lose your respect for him? Haven't you yourself ever been in a situation where you felt yourself close to tears?

Stand in front of the faded original of our Declaration of Independence in Washington. Look up at the brooding statue of our Civil War President inside the Lincoln Memorial. Lay your hand on the Liberty Bell in Philadelphia. Walk across Concord Bridge and stand beside the Minute Man. Find yourself blinking to keep the tears back? The associations brought to mind by these objects arouse a flood of emotions that simply demands an outlet. The easiest by far is tears.

Tears aren't always triggered by sorrow, sympathy, grief or a train of thought. Sometimes sheer beauty is enough to bring on an outburst. The late Charles Laughton was once at Chapel Hill to give a program of readings at the University of North Carolina. Walking through the university gardens that afternoon, he came upon a bank of massed daffodils and narcissuses. The sight was so movingly beautiful that Laughton burst into tears.

History records famous men who wept in public. Alexander the Great wept because there were no more worlds for him to conquer. Scipio spoke of "the gracious gift of tears." Abraham Lincoln was proud of his ability to weep for relief and in sympathy, and what Bible reader does not know that Jesus wept.

In our own time, too, outstanding men shed tears in public. Generalissimo Chiang Kai-shek wept at the funeral of one of his generals. General George Patton, after his victory in Europe, wept at a testimonial dinner tendered him in Boston. Even rugged John L. Lewis shed tears as he took his United Mine Workers Union out of the C.I.O.

When TV great Arthur Godfrey fired his star singer, Julius LaRosa, both men shed tears while discussing the affair with reporters. Godfrey wept on another occasion—when he described over coast-to-coast radio the funeral of President Franklin D. Roosevelt. Godfrey was frankly crying as he spoke. No one in America thought less of him.

Only a few years ago, when General Dean was liberated from a North Korean prisoner-of-war camp, he washed away the humiliation and suffering of those years with unrestrained, unashamed tears. Perhaps the greatest humanitarian of our century, Dr. Albert Schweitzer, was known to weep in public.

So next time you feel close to tears, let 'em come. You'll be better off for it. After all, why be a tough guy with a mixed-up inside when it's just as easy to be a little less tough with a well-adjusted inside?

Know what happens when you tie down the safety valve on a steam engine? The whole thing may blow up. So don't tie down the safety valve on your emotions. Shed a tear if the occasion demands. You may actually be helping yourself live a longer, a happier and a better-adjusted life!

The next time you reach for a cocktail,
stop and ask yourself if there isn't
a sign before you that reads . . .

DANGER! ALCOHOLISM AHEAD

by LILA LENNON

Yes—You *can* become an alcoholic. In fact, if you have already stepped over the thin line that separates the regular social drinker from the *alcohol-dependent* drinker, you may be in danger of taking the next, very short step towards becoming a victim of that incurable disease known as alcoholism.

It can happen to anyone—rich or poor, educated or illiterate, young or old—the more than five million alcoholics in the U.S. come from all levels of society and economic status, from all occupations.

It is estimated that about 71 per cent of the population drinks, and that one out of fifteen people will end up as an alcoholic. That one person is, or will become, an alcohol-dependent drinker. Usually, he is not even aware that his drinking has reached this dangerous, pre-alcoholic stage and does not suspect that for him disaster is just around the next corner.

What causes that one person out of fifteen to step into the abyss of excessive, repetitive and uncontrolled drinking? Prevailing scientific opinion is that a combination of physical, psychological and environmental factors are involved, and that alcoholism is in the man—or woman—not in the bottle.

Unfortunately, most people are likely to resent being told they're "drinking too much" and, in addition, they also develop a kind of protective amnesia about how often and how much they drink. Even those who consider themselves just "social drinkers" frequently remain unaware of increased consumption, but the answer is easily obtainable—simply by marking every drink, each day, on a calendar pad for a month. The total may prove to be shocking—and sobering.

For a majority, social drinking creates no problems and does not disrupt their lives in any way; it is the alcohol-dependent drinker who is most likely to acquire the serious, complex disease of alcoholism, and it is a grim fact that 10 per cent of the adult population *are* alcohol-dependent drinkers.

How can you tell how far or how fast you're traveling along the downhill road to alcohol dependency? Your answer to the following questions will help you spot signs that spell *Danger!*

How long have you been drinking?

How much do you drink?

How often?

When?

Why?

Has the amount and frequency of your drinking increased?

Do you feel you cannot have a good time without a drink—that it's a "must"for all social encounters, including golf, fishing, card playing, etc."

Has the "martini luncheon" become a daily fact of life as a means of selling either your products or services?

Do you anticipate having a drink immediately after work?

Do you make a point of stopping at a bar or heading for the bar car on the train before going home?

Do you have a definite tendency to drink on "signal"—before luncheon, dinner or bedtime to celebrate something or for other "special" reasons?

Do you drink every day, for one or more of the following reasons—to erase fatigue, to alleviate boredom, frustration, anxiety or discouragement?

If your answers give you an uneasy feeling that it's time to turn off that downhill road, you can take the following "detours":

Keep an accurate, truthful record of the number of drinks you take.

Never take a drink *every* day.

Don't drink on an empty stomach.

If you feel you "need" a drink—don't take it. Substitute walking, for instance, (and for miles, if necessary) for the drink.

Space your drinks. Don't take (or as a guest accept) the second drink for a half hour after you've finished the first. Allow an hour before taking the third, and don't take the fourth.

Dilute the amount of alcohol by sticking to long, weak drinks.

Break the habit of drinking "on signal"—substitute hot strong tea or bouillon before meals, warm cocoa or other caffeine-free beverages before bed.

When you feel especially tired or tense, substitute the hot-tub-soak and cold-shower routine for a drink.

Never, *never* drink in the morning to "overcome" a hangover.

In addition, a frank discussion with your doctor or clergyman, or both, can be helpful in learning how to find other detours that lead away from the road to alcohol dependency.

The alcohol-dependent drinker is already on the downhill road that can, and will for some, lead to the dead-end street of broken dreams, hopes and lives. But the danger signs are there, if you will slow down, read them . . . and heed them!

Since three minutes of anger will sap
your strength quicker than eight hours of work . . .

CAN YOU AFFORD YOUR TEMPER?

by DUANE VALENTRY

Bill Hamilton's job never looked so good as it did the day he walked out the door for the last time. He had one consolation. "Well, I finally told that guy off!"

But this was small comfort. Nor did it stack up well against the necessity of telling the wife she'd have to cut corners until he came up with something.

Bill's temper had cost him another job, his chances of becoming sales manager and his peace of mind. He decided this last blowup had been a lot more expensive than it was worth.

Can you afford your temper? Temper can be the most expensive thing in your life. Ask Bill Hamilton, or the man eating his heart out with remorse in jail because in a fit of rage he broke his crying child's arm. Ask the woman who flares up and loses friends faster than she can make them.

Many unhappy marriages result from the uncontrolled temper of a marriage partner. One man didn't like the way his wife cooked dinner and threw it at her: another raged because his wife spent too much on clothes and ripped everything in her closet.

Childish? Unreasoning? Temper usually is. Even when justified, it's costly to the indulger, according to doctors, psychiatrists and temper-indulgers themselves.

"What I need is to belong to a 'Tempers Anonymous,' an organization like the one drinkers have," says a man with a cocked-trigger temper.

A bad temper is a burden to the one possessing it and to

those around him. Like the drinker, he is often a fine person otherwise, intelligent and affectionate, which is why temper has been called the "vice of the virtuous."

Again, like the drinker, he suffers remorse and self-condemnation, often to an agonizing degree. He swears to reform, never to let himself go again and, like the drinker, he doesn't until next time.

The bad-tempered man apologized for his actions to those he has offended and tries to make up to friends for things he has said and done. Often, because they're friends, they forgive him. But temper has broken many friendships.

Probably more importantly, he can't forgive himself. Each letting-go takes something from him and adds a sickness of soul which is part of the high price of temper. But it is costly to health, too.

"Three minutes of anger will sap your strength quicker than eight hours of work," says the Reverend Charles W. Shedd, who has counseled many burdened with this problem. "Why? Because it has put a terrific strain on your body. When you are angry, your blood rushes to the major muscles of arms and legs. Thus you have greater physical strength, but your brain, lacking its full blood supply, is cut down in efficiency. This is why you say things you do not mean and do things which seem outlandish."

This is similar to "euphoria," which causes one under the influence of alcohol to do things he will look back on with regret.

Doctors know many of the body's ills come from attitudes of anger, hate and resentment, and that many a sick man or woman recovers by the simple process of substituting patience for impatience, calmness for anger, and love for hate.

Few psychiatrists today tell troubled patients to blow their tops if they feel like it. Such temporary release, they have found, lacks the curative power of replacing hate with love.

"Why keep giving in to a bad habit?" asks Dr. Walter Alvarez, formerly of the Mayo Clinic, in his syndicated medical column. "That only helps it to fasten itself upon you. Fight the habit every day, and eventually you will be free of it, and hence so much nicer a person."

Thousands know the terrible cost of temper to peace of mind. "I'll regret to my dying day the mean things I said to my Dad in an argument—I never had a chance to say I was sorry, he went so quickly," young Fred Nelson commented sadly at his father's funeral.

Anger costs the co-operation and good opinions of others, as well as their affection and regard. Like alcoholism it needs to be faced to be cured.

"We had personnel trouble in our office and lost valuable work time through turnover," relates a once-choleric boss. "Nobody would take my fits of anger very long. I had to get myself in hand—home life has become happier, too."

Temper robs a woman of beauty and a man of dignity. Helen of Troy could not look beautiful in a rage as actress Ava Gardner proved recently when she threw champagne at photographers.

"It is no sin to have a temper, only to go on having it and prayer has helped many to bring a bad temper under control," recommends the Reverend Charles W. Shedd. "The best way to lose your temper is to lose yourself in God."

Physical action also helps. Breaking something or running around the block works off adrenaline in the system, with no cost involved.

"Every time you get into an argument you have a small chance of boosting your ego and softening the opposition and a big chance of losing a friend and hardening an artery," says Mary Martin, Broadway star, who goes out of her way to avoid a discordant situation.

Self-analysis helps. If temper fits follow a pattern they can be forestalled. Anger may come with fatigue, a let-down or with worry; and half the battle is won if such tendencies are recognized.

John Hudson got in a bad temper at the end of the day when he had to buck traffic and "all those fool drivers." Then he tried calming his thoughts, to think of the other drivers as men like himself, going home. Trying earnestly to "get close to God," before long Hudson was enjoying the trip home and was heard to remark to his wife that traffic had changed a lot. It hadn't; he had.

Henry Drummond's famous essay, The Greatest Thing in the

World," which has helped many overcome tempers, warns that the Bible "again and again returns to condemn it (anger) as one of the most destructive elements in human nature.

"No form of vice, not worldliness, not greed of gold, not drunkenness itself," said Drummond, "does more to un-Christianize society than evil temper. For embittering life; for breaking up communities; for destroying the most sacred relationships; for devastating homes; for withering up men and women; for taking the bloom of childhood; in short, for sheer gratuitous misery-producing power, this influence stands alone."

The price of temper is so high, who can afford it?

8
OPPORTUNITY
UNLIMITED

*A wise man will make more
opportunities than he finds.*
–Francis Bacon

*He was a pioneer in his field
and his writings became . . .*

A MIRACLE OF POSITIVE THINKING

by WILLIAM L. ROPER

"Since 1892, I've had nothing to do, do ...do ... do ..."

While thousands of idle discouraged Americans chanted this ditty of defeatism during the devastating panic of 1893-98—a time of riots, hunger marches and threats of revolution—one American was busy working on a "success" book that was to bring new hope to millions and play an important role in restoring prosperity to America.

His name was Orison Swett Marden. The book, the first of more than forty he devoted to the theme of winning personal success by positive thinking and self-discipline, was *Pushing to the Front.*

Early in life, Marden, an orphan at seven, had read Dr. Samuel Smile's book *Self-Help,* and decided there must be a formula for achievement. Later, in seeking the reasons why some men achieve greatness and wealth despite all kinds of obstacles he interviewed Thomas A. Edison, John D. Rockefeller, Andrew Carnegie, Alexander Graham Bell and other successful men.

Marden's research convinced him that there were certain basic rules for accomplishment: self confidence; positive, creative thinking; hard work; concentrated effort; singleness of purpose and clean living. Other men before Marden had discovered these virtues, but he was one of the first to formulate them into a pattern for successful living.

Today the value of these rules for mental discipline is widely recognized. And they are just as useful now as they were then. By applying them, young persons today have a definite advantage over those who think one must have a barrel of luck or a magic pull to win.

Marden's own life demonstrated the truth of his success philosophy.

One night in 1892, just as the great Depression was getting under way, Marden's Midway Hotel in Kearney, Nebraska, burned to the ground. With it was burned the manuscript of his "success" book, *Pushing to the Front.*

The loss was a severe blow to his dwindling fortune, acquired by careful saving and prudent investment. But what grieved him far more was the destruction of his manuscript.

What would he do now? Even before the embers stopped smoking, Marden made up his mind.

Renting a barren room over a livery stable, Marden started to work, rewriting his book. That winter he lived on $1.50 a week. He was sustained by his enormous self-confidence and faith in his idea, although the clouds of the coming Depression grew darker.

For years he had studied and analyzed the techniques used by so-called self-made men in attaining success. He was convinced others could use the same methods effectively. That was the purpose of his book—to show young men and women how to make their dreams come true. Its theme, stated simply, was: "He can who thinks he can."

Marden was deeply in debt when spring came. Manfully, he struggled to complete the book. Meanwhile, the soup lines in the big cities grew longer, and panic mounted.

When Marden offered his "success" book to publishers, they rejected it. Some countered: "How can people buy books when they can't buy bread?"

Marden realized now that all of the rules he had formulated for overcoming obstacles and achieving success were faced with a decisive test. One of the chapters in his book was about "Grit" and the courage to carry on despite difficulties. Marden had those qualities.

He recalled Mirabeau's classic phrase: "Nothing is impossible to the man who can will."

And Marden himself had written: "The strong-willed, intelligent, persistent man will find or make a way where, in the nature of things, a way can be found or made."

So packing a suitcase with his few possessions, including the manuscript of his precious book, he left Kearney for Chicago in 1893.

There he found temporary employment as manager of the Park Gate Hotel during the World's Columbian Exposition. When off duty, he visited local publishers, trying to persuade one to publish his book. None would risk it.

A few days after the Fair closed, Marden journeyed to Boston where he had friends. It was there he had received his B.A. degree from Boston University in 1877 and an M.D. from Harvard in 1882.

But business conditions in Boston weren't much better than in Chicago. That was the spring that Jacob S. Coxey led his army of twenty thousand unemployed, half-starved men in a march on Washington. Pessimism reigned. America was in the doldrums. Businessmen hesitated to try new ventures. Hoarding was common.

How could America be saved and business rejuvenated? A few political leaders advocated a foreign war. Others proposed doles.

Then, in 1894, a miracle happened. Marden, with the aid of friends who were impressed by the merit of his idea and his own unshaken faith in it, got his book published. The first edition of *Pushing to the Front* sold out quickly. A second went equally fast. In spite of hard times, people were finding money to buy the book.

For panic-sick America, the volume's courageous, optimistic philosophy was just what the doctor ordered. It gave the discouraged new hope, new faith in themselves. Undoubtedly, it helped to change the mental outlook of thousands, and so became a turning point in the nation's economy.

Eventually, the book went through 250 editions and was translated into many foreign languages. In Japan and several other foreign countries, it was used extensively in the public schools. Queen Victoria wrote a letter commending it.

Marden followed *Pushing to the Front* with other books based on the same general theme: *Rising in the World* (1896), *Every Man a King* (1906), *The Optimistic Life* (1907), *He Can Who Thinks He Can* (1908), *Everybody Ahead* (1917), *Ambition and Success*

(1919) and *Masterful Personality* (1921). In 1911, he brought out a new and enlarged edition of *Pushing to the Front.* It continued to be a best seller.

Thirty of his books were translated into German and more than three million of them were sold in twenty-five languages.

There is an inspiration in Marden's life as well as in the books he wrote. Born near Thornton, New Hampshire, in 1850, he became self-supporting at an early age. While attending Boston University and later at Harvard, he waited on tables and developed a catering business to pay his way. He had saved nearly $20,000 before completing college. With this nest egg, he bought an old tourist hotel on Block Island, off Newport, Rhode Island, and by intelligent promotion developed his holdings until he owned controlling interests in five hotels, including the Midland in Kearney. With the Depression, his hotel business collapsed and he was near bankruptcy when the Midland burned that night in 1892.

In addition to writing books, Marden was publishing a successful national magazine when he died on March 10, 1924.

By his own yardstick, he was a success. In *Rising in the World,* he had written: "The greatest thing a man can do in this world is to make the most possible out of the stuff that has been given him. This is success, and there is no other."

Marden made the most of what he had, using one theme as the basis for forty books. And in a period of tight money, his first book had become a best seller. Even more importantly he helped to inspire a nation at a time when the gospel of positive, courageous thinking was desperately needed.

Stop and think! Isn't it time for you to . . .

GET OFF THE TREADMILL!

by W. CLEMENT STONE

Centuries ago in China there was a great drought. Rice then, as it is now was the staple food of the Chinese. It was also a medium of exchange. It was money. The rice fields were dying with thirst. Without rain to water them, there would be famine, sickness, even death for the people.

A young farmer whose name has long been forgotten was sitting on a river bank. This young man was the father of three children—all with beautiful brown eyes. He was the husband of a woman who shared all he had, including labor in the field. He had just returned from the village shrine where he had prayed for hours—for rain.

As he sat on the ledge looking at the water of the winding river, the stories told to him by his grandfather kept bothering him—stories of the great drought of another generation. Hundreds of thousands of people died because of famine. This young man wanted his wife and children to live. He, too, wanted to live.

What could he do? With the flash of inspiration that comes from a burning desire—or could it have been an answer to his prayers?—he had a vision.

This young Chinese had a treadmill that was propelled by an ox. When the animal walked, he was forced to move in a circle as the outside of the wheel turned. In his mind's eye, the farmer pictured two large wheels supported by an axle in a horizontal position. Boards were firmly attached as steps between these two wheels. A series of buckets hung on the outside of one wheel. These buckets would scoop up water from the river as the treadmill, in turning, rose from its lowest point. They would dump the water into a trough that would carry it to the rice field as the wheel revolved downward from its highest position.

He was unable to visualize his ox treading such a contraption. "I would do the work of an ox to save my family," he thought. Then he got into action! He called together a group of farmers, all of whom were faced with the same problem. He explained his plan. Together they made treadmills that brought the water from the river to the rice fields above. Since that time, there hasn't been a famine because of lack of rain.

Centuries ago, the treadmill was an invention of great benefit. But what about today? Men or women in many parts of the world are still doing the work of an animal on the same type of treadmill invented by a young Chinese farmer who was a benefactor to his people. Hour after hour—day after day—step by step—they tread.

To the traveler, this sight is interesting, strange and picturesque. Yet in this modern machine age, such wearisome, endless toil seems needless.

Perhaps you are on a treadmill—not one that raises water from a river to the rice fields above, but one just as wearisome, just as needless and far more frustrating. You might say to the wife of the Chinese farmer: "Get off the treadmill!" Yet in his wisdom, the Chinese farmer might respond: "Why don't you get off your treadmill?" Perhaps you and the Chinese farmer would find it just as easy or just as hard. Why? You would need to take time to stop and think. You may need to develop self-motivation. You may need to develop a burning desire. With these, you could find the way.

Just like the young Chinese farmer whose name has long been forgotten, you too can . . . *get off the treadmill!*

Miracles begin to happen when you
change your I Can't philosophy
to I Can.

A HOME FOR TEN CENTS

by BEN SWEETLAND

John Doyce was forty-five years old. He was a house painter, married, the father of two children. He was working in my living room when he paused, turned to me and said, "You don't know how lucky you are. I'd give anything to have a home of my own."

"Why don't you?" I asked.

John looked at me with an expression which clearly indicated his surprise that I should ask such a seemingly nonsensical question. Laying his brush down and leaning against his ladder, he spent fully five minutes telling me why he did not own a home. I was reminded of the cost of bringing up two children; how hard youngsters are on their clothes; the inevitability of bills for the doctor and medicine; the high and rising cost of living. He considered himself lucky and a good manager to come out even at the end of the month, let alone purchase a home.

Having felt I was properly put in my place, John picked up his brush and continued the rhythmic swing right and left as he brought freshness to the walls.

While my painter friend continued his occupation of surface transformation, I picked up an empty candy box and, with the aid of adhesive tape, bound the cover so that it could not be removed and with my pocket knife carved a neat slot in the top of the box, giving it the appearance of a small savings bank. Then, with my ball-point pen, I lettered neatly on the side of the box: "Building Fund."

Noon arrived, and after John Doyce had squatted on the

floor with his lunch box between his legs, I approached him with a question quite provocative. "Let me have a coin—any coin," I commanded. Reaching down in his pocket he produced an array of small change, pennies, a nickel or two, a dime, etc. I reached over, picked up a ten-cent piece from his hand and dropped it through the slot in my improvised bank.

Almost with the ceremony of laying a cornerstone, I presented the box to the puzzled painter with the statement: "John, with this important step you have just taken, the home of your dreams is now on its way."

I didn't give him a chance for questioning, but for several minutes I held the floor with a flow of logic he could not dispute.

Saving is a habit—just as spending is a habit. The one who acquires a habit of saving will find it just as easy to adjust his expenditures so that a portion of every paycheck is saved, as the opposite type will find it seemingly necessary to spend every penny received.

John was told that every time he got any money at all, he was to take some of it, if only the tiniest portion, and put it in the box. He did admit that he could do this, but his attitude expressed his doubt that such dribbles would ever amount to anything of importance, especially a sum which could figure in the purchase of a house.

It would have been appropriate to revert to the timeworn illustration, "Mighty oaks from little acorns grow." But I am sure John, with his quizzical mind, would have told me that he would not want to wait the length of time normally required to convert an acorn into a mighty oak.

Houses are built by placing brick upon brick or board upon board. They do not come into being instantly, as if through the wave of a magic wand. The completed structure represents a myriad of small operations. As in travel, regardless of the distance, it must be covered mile by mile.

In my busy life, counselling with people constantly, both personally and via television and radio, it is simple and quite natural to lose touch with individual cases. This was true so far as John Doyce was concerned. He had slipped my mind completely—until the mailman handed me a neatly printed invitation to a house-warming—and, to my pleased amazement it was for the new home of Mr. and Mrs. John Doyce.

It was a charming home, quite modern. The large living room had its dining area adjacent to a glamourous kitchen which would arouse the envy of most housewives. There was a master bedroom and two of the most interesting rooms for the children. The center of activity for the house-warming was in the rumpus room—or what is now frequently referred to as the social hall.

It was a long time before I gained the opportunity of congratulating this proud home owner. He and his happy wife were busily engaged in conducting tours of inspection through the newly acquired domicile.

Finally, literally grabbing John by the arm, I sat him down at a table on the terrace, and I relaxed as he unfolded a story which proved highly inspirational, even though it was based on fundamentals I knew so well.

The most interesting part of John's story was not what you might expect, how pennies grow into dollars, dollars into tens, tens into hundreds and hundreds into thousands.

"My greatest victory," exclaimed Doyce thoughtfully, "was learning that *I Can* instead of *I Can't.*"

He continued, "Up to the time I worked in your home, I was definitely certain a home was for the other fellow, not for me. Living from pay-day to pay-day without having a cent saved, your query as to why I didn't own a home came as a paradox. We are not extravagant. We had always felt we lived modestly so that to save for a home, as I thought at that time, would have meant a sacrifice too great to impose upon my family."

Determination to accomplish does not always imply sacrifice. It calls into play one's resourcefulness to augment his present income—thereby enabling him to reach his objective. As this painter saw his spare change growing into bankbook figures, his enthusiasm mounted to such an extent that he sought overtime work. And since he had been able to live and save on his regular income, he wisely took the entire proceeds of his extra work and added it to his now established building fund. Of course, such a move on his part caused his savings curve to ascend abruptly.

The head of a family recently told me that the very high price of steaks and meat in general caused him to live on less money. The family budget, being too small to permit the luxury of fillets and prime roasts, forced his wife to call upon her ingenuity in preparing tasty dishes from less expensive items of food. Stews, with an abundance of nourishing vegetables, were often found on the menu. The less expensive fowl supplied many tasty, satisfying meals. Instead of too frequent pots of dollar-a-pound coffee, the family found it was helping the nervous system by using less of the enchanting beverage.

The Doyce family followed this sound pattern in meal planning, which added more speed to the mounting building fund. And as the rejoicing husband told me, they were actually living better than they had been before. This is understandable when we realize that merely tossing a steak into the broiler takes much less mental effort than planning a meal requiring combinations of many ingredients.

Since this objective has been attained, will the Doyce family revert to their former living patterns? No sir-e-e! Buying his home is merely the beginning. They have started another building fund—this one to enable them to acquire a piece of income property, a house of two or more rentable flats. "And that is not all," he added almost boastfully. "After I get my income property, I'm going into the painting contracting business for myself and have others working for me, instead of being dependent on others for a job."

"What's this?" I asked as I was preparing to leave the memorable housewarming. I was looking at an interesting plaque built into a niche in the entrance hall. Inlaid in a polished piece of walnut burl was a dime and around it were engraved the words: "The Foundation on Which This Home Was Built."

My thoughts went back to the workman painting the walls in my home who so solemnly said: "I'd give anything to own a home of my own."

When was the last time you
tried to punch a hole in the sky?

MAKE THE IMPOSSIBLE YOUR GOAL!

by DR. HAROLD BLAKE WALKER

Test pilots, punching into the stratosphere, climbing to undreamed heights in jet and rocket planes, have a phrase they use to describe their work.

They call it "punching holes in the sky."

That is what we were meant to do with our lives, to climb beyond humdrum, reach up beyond preoccupation with gadgets and things, press on beyond "the little aims that end with self."

We aim too low. When it comes to living, we are masters of the mediocre, satisfied with good enough. After all, we are human, we tell ourselves. We are reasonably respectable, by the world's standards. Maybe we are a bit selfish and more than a little stubborn, but so is everybody else we know. Maybe we have prejudices and jaundiced opinions, but who doesn't?

The ideals of the Divine adventure seem quite impossible. The sky is too high to think of punching holes in it. It is the impossible that stops us. But nonetheless it is the challenge of the impossible that gets life out of its rut and onto a highway that goes somewhere. It makes life interesting and thoroughly worth living.

So a weary, weatherbeaten collection of acrobats learned when their act was falling flat. Bosley Crowther describes how they tried to coax a little laughter and applause from a vaudeville audience with their stale routine. Then one of them came down to the footlights and, in a voice that betrayed grim despair, announced to the audience: "We will now do a trick that's impossible."

Thereupon his fellows leaped to frightening perches, the audience woke up, the top man clapped his hands with bristling confidence . . . and out went the lights. When the lights came on, the smiling acrobats were posing proudly in the center of the ring, the impossible quite obviously accomplished. The audience gave them a big hand.

The lights did not go out in the first century when a strange collection of men and women challenged the shoddy standards of the Roman Empire in the name of an "impossible" dream called Christianity. Strange, too, how humanity woke up when they got busy "punching holes in the sky" and began to upset the world.

To be sure, Rome was not built in a day, and life becomes neither a spiritual success nor a moral failure overnight. Thomas a Kempis had it right when he wrote: "If every year we would root out one vice, we would soon become perfect."

That may be overoptimistic, but at least there is a kernel of truth in it. And when you get at the business of punching holes in your little two-by-four sky, anything can happen. The Wright brothers managed to fly a hundred feet off the ground, and that seemed like a miracle. Then we thought the sky really had been pierced when we got to five thousand feet. Now we crash through sixty thousand feet and know we have by no means reached the limit.

Start with yourself as you are and root out the worst in yourself. Maybe you have a long way to climb, but you have to start somewhere. Possibly you have a stubborn streak that makes you a problem at home, in the office or even in your club. Start there and see what God can do with your stubbornness. Get Him into your thinking when you are standing sternly for your own way and making everybody miserable.

Don't be disappointed if you can't overhaul yourself from top to bottom overnight. There is more than a hint of warning in the comment of an illiterate farmer intent on learning to read and write. After some study, he took his pencil and began scribbling. Suddenly he shouted to his wife: "Maria, come here. I can write." She looked at his doodling and said: "Wonderful. What does it say?" "One thing at a time," he said, "I haven't learned how to read yet."

Start where you are, with the things in you that sometimes make you hate yourself. Take one thing at a time, and put God's strength beside your own weakness. The only true failure lies in failure to start.

At the very least, you can be better than you are if you have the wit to reach beyond your grasp and faith enough to believe you can be what you ought to be.

9
SALES UNLIMITED

Sales are contingent upon the attitude of the salesman—not the attitude of the prospect.
                    –W. Clement Stone

It's great to be a president of a corporation (or an executive in a responsible position) . . . if you can take it. Perhaps you can. Perhaps you can't. But this article may help you crystallize your thinking about yourself. It may motivate you to higher achievement or give you ideas for a healthier, happier mental attitude toward your present work, your present position and the jobs you might like to hold in the future. For many of the principles are applicable to all those who hope to be, or are, in a position of leadership.

REMINISCING . . .
FROM NEWSBOY TO PRESIDENT

By W. CLEMENT STONE

At the age of six I sold newspapers at 31st and Cottage Grove in the city of Chicago. Today I am president of Combined Insurance Company of America, each of its subsidiaries and several other organizations. And there is a relationship between the newsboy and the president: experience, know-how and sales activity knowledge.

The saying "a salesman is born . . . not made" is a fallacy, as any successful sales manager should know. And it is also true: a successful president or executive, teacher, lawyer, doctor, inventor, scientist, philosopher, artist or genius is not born . . . he, too, is made. Self-made. And each is measured by the results he obtains . . . his achievements.

For every *normal* person is endowed with great mental capacities. Few use and develop their natural abilities sufficiently to reach the many goals they could achieve. And this applies to all of us. But we can develop our abilities more fully in the future if we are motivated to pay the price. We can begin right now . . . to develop the *want-to* (self-motivation), learn the *know-how* (experience) and acquire the necessary *activity knowledge*.

The price? Regular investment in *study, thinking and planning time*, followed through with action . . . *work*. But with proper motivation, know-how, activity knowledge and achievement, work becomes fun. This I learned from experience.

As a newsboy I learned a lot that helped me later as a salesman, sales manager and executive, even though I didn't realize it at the time. I know now that I began to learn then that if I couldn't solve a problem one way, I could another. Thus that first day when I tried to sell papers at 31st and Cottage Grove, a then busy business intersection, the newsboys who were older and bigger than I beat me up to keep me from interfering with their sales. That's why I walked into Hoelle's Restaurant and completely sold out my stock of papers. This eventually led me to realize that every disadvantage can be turned to an advantage if one tries to solve his problem.

Also as a newsboy I began to learn how to overcome fear . . . through action; the value of persistence when it made sales; and how to sell by using a method others were afraid to use: cold-canvassing, that is, calling on business people in business places without an introduction. That's the way I sold insurance. And that's the reason I sold as many accident policies in a single week as many insurance men sell over a period of many months. Why?

As a newsboy I was motivated by necessity. I had borrowed the money to buy the papers. I had to sell them to repay the loan and make a profit. Also as a salesman, a sales manager and an executive, necessity has become a wholesome motivating factor in the solution of problems. Many of the principles I learned selling newspapers between the ages of six and thirteen I have been able to apply in my business activities in adult life. Here are a few examples, followed by statements of the principles involved.

The success in selling newspapers in Hoelle's Restaurant on the first day was repeated day after day. Also, in developing a system for the sale of accident and health insurance, I did that which most insurance men didn't do: at the time of the renewal of a policy I did not merely send a notice but I personally called on each client to renew. Thus I guaranteed the renewal, sold additional protection when needed by my client and increased my number of customers in his place of business.

Determine the principles which bring success and those which bring failure. Employ the principles that bring success, and avoid those which bring failure.

At the age of twelve I entered a hospital to try to sell my

papers by calling room to room. I reasoned that the patients would make good prospects and I could see a lot of persons in a short space of time. Because I sold more papers per hour of effort through this experience than any other, I repeated it daily. And in later years, as an insurance salesman, I used exactly the same principle in selling to employees, during business hours, in the largest banks, department stores, government buildings, railway offices, hospitals and other institutions in the United States.

> *Relate, assimilate and use principles that are successful in one activity . . . in related activities.*
>
> *Sell in large institutions where . . . others are afraid to sell.*
>
> *Make greater profits in less selling time by concentrating your efforts in an area where there are a large number of prospects, and thus eliminate waste in travel time.*
>
> *Go where the money is.*
>
> *Where there is nothing to lose by trying, and a great deal to gain if successful, by all means try.*

And I learned something else by selling newspapers in the hospital. When I started I thought the patients would be there for several days, so I began to make collections once a week. But I soon found that many of my patients didn't stay an entire week. So I collected daily. Also my profits increased because of daily gratuities rather than weekly. Perhaps collecting for the newspapers at the time of delivery is one of the reasons why I later, in selling insurance, made it a practice to collect the premium at the time of application.

> *Get your money at the time of sale.*

At the age of seven or eight, I liked movies, and I probably saw more movies than any youngster I have ever known. There was a large movie house at 31st and Prairie near the apartment where we lived, and a smaller one five blocks west of us. At the larger theater the management, to get business, gave each paying customer a white ticket. The white ticket gave admission to the balcony seats for the following evening. So I would wait outside the theater for the white ticket someone might not want.

Now the smaller theater competed by allowing children free if accompanied by their parents. I went in as a child of couples of all ages. As I look back, I think the owner knew, for he never said anything and didn't allow any of his employees to stop the practice.

As a salesman selling in large establishments, I obtained permission to sell from the owner by asking him for permission. He had nothing to lose; his employees and I had a lot to gain.

If a person has nothing to lose by giving, and you have lots to gain by asking, give him the opportunity to grant you the favor that costs him nothing.

Now of course, I didn't understand these principles as a newsboy. And as a salesman while I was searching to develop a success formula, I didn't realize that I was using many of the same principles I had employed in my first business venture, selling newspapers. Even when I established my own insurance agency at the age of twenty, and later trained salesmen to use those techniques I had found successful in my personal selling, I wasn't aware of the relationship. The discovery of the connection between the principles used in my early experiences and those I subsequently had, became crystal clear when I worked on the manuscript for my book, *The Success System That Never Fails.*

"President" is defined as the chief officer of a corporation, society or the like. A man in business for himself has the same responsibility as the president of a corporation.

In a sense a foreman, department head, superintendent, sales manager or officer of a company has many of the responsibilities of a president or the owner of a business, even though the area of responsibility is smaller. As an individual, to be successful he must employ the same basic principles that are necessary for success in the job he has; also in preparation for the promotion he would like to achieve. And this is true of a salesman, office employee or laborer.

For every individual must start with himself. He must be self-made. Therefore it is desirable to motivate ourselves to higher achievement and continually to search for ideas that will bring about a healthier, happier mental attitude towards our present work, our present position and those positions we might like to hold in the future. The basic principles are applicable to everyone. And in the end our success will be evaluated by results—our achievements.

10
SUCCESS UNLIMITED

Success is achieved and maintained
by those who try—and keep trying.
—W. Clement Stone

Can success be reduced to a formula? Are there qualities and principles that are always present in truly successful individuals? Analyze this article and those to follow and then decide for yourself.

THE INGREDIENTS OF SUCCESS

by LARSTON D. FARRAR

Some years ago, the late B. C. Forbes, publisher of *Forbes—Magazine of Business* put a team of business reporters to work interviewing the men who had been chosen, in nationwide balloting among businessmen, as the fifty foremost business leaders of that period.

The result was a popular book, *America's Fifty Foremost Business Leaders,* published in 1948.

As one of the team, I interviewed some of the most prominent men in American life—the men at the top of the heap. They included Walter C. Carpenter, chairman of E.I. du Pont de Nemours & Company, Ernest E. Norris, president of the Southern Railway System, and Edgar Queeny, chairman of Monsanto Chemical Company.

At the "Fifty-Foremost" banquet in the grand ballroom of the Waldorf-Astoria Hotel in New York, I had the honor of meeting most of them personally. It was an experience I shall never forget.

For a long time, I have been striving to put my finger on the qualities these men possessed in common. I wanted to isolate, if possible, the factors that make for success, so as to achieve it myself, as well as pass the magic words on to others who might be striving for the heights.

One point early came to my mind. It is that these men were *lucky* in one vital respect—they had been able to exercise their talents in a unique land, the United States of America. Joel Barlow, an early America, said in the seventeenth century: "If ever virtue is to be rewarded, it will be in America."

I observed many traits in common among the fifty foremost American businessmen indicating they had attained "virtue."

For one thing, I observed that they invariably were men of *humility*.

It may seem odd, to some, that "big" men should feel more humble than many workers in the mills, mines and factories the leaders control. Yet I was reminded of what Jesus said when He pointed out that if a man wants to be a master, he first must become a servant. Jesus washed the feet of His disciples to show His own humility. Yet they accepted Him as their master.

Every one of these men—even those who were some of the founders and later inherited stock ownership of an industry—had served long years of apprenticeship in the ranks of the businesses they headed. Most of them started out on the lowest rung. They had learned, by experience, *every phase* of the businesses they now were directing. They had opportunity to study people on every tier of society. Apparently the "higher" they went, the more humble they became. Perhaps their knowledge made them realize more poignantly their dependence on other individuals who operate their vast companies.

"I am one of the least useful persons on this railroad," Ernest Norris, then president of the Southern Railway System, told me. "As far as the public is concerned, this railroad is the conductor who takes up the tickets and either smiles or frowns while he does it. If a piece of freight is crushed through carelessness, it might inconvenience a customer, so the most menial loader on a freight platform is more important, to the customer, than I am at any particular time. At all times, I am dependent on every man who works on this railroad—from the vice-president, who may transmit my order to the porter who may ruin a man's trunk through careless handling. The higher you go in business, the more you realize *your own dependence* on other human beings."

A part of the innate humility of these men was the recognition that they did not "know it all." Another thread which I observed running through the lives of every one of them was a sincere search for knowledge. I was amazed to learn that one of the men I interviewed was taking an evening course in sociology. Cautioning me not to mention it, he told me he had always wanted to learn more about the subject, but that through the years he had been so busy he hadn't had time for it. Now one of the most successful men in the country, he still was studying and learning.

And why not? Hadn't he—and had not all the others—achieved their goals by learning that the joy is in the doing? Men who win prizes realize, after they have the cups sitting on the mantel, that the greatest thrills came to them not while they were collecting the prizes, but when they were playing the game, running the race or doing their jobs. It seems to me that these men all had learned, in varying degrees, that the joy of life is in the doing of things that prepared them to do bigger things on a different level.

Another quality that seemed to run like a strand through all the fifty leaders was *patience*. They had learned, I could tell in the little things they did, not to be impatient either with themselves or with others. They realized that delays, difficulties, mishaps and circumstances are a part and parcel of life in this or any civilization.

On one occasion, while I was interviewing Edgar Queeny, chairman of Monsanto Chemical, he buzzed for his secretary. She apparently had gone out on an errand, for there was no answer. Because he wanted to get some information from the files for me, he excused himself, smiling. When he returned with the file in his hand, he explained, still smiling:

"The situation is rather hectic around here today. We're having a special surprise party later for one of the officials. He's going to take charge of one of our plants. I imagine that preparations were too much for my personal staff today."

He wasn't at all perturbed because no one answered his buzz, although normally several attachés listen for it.

My questioning of associates and coworkers among the fifty foremost business leaders indicated to me that these men were noted among subordinates for their patience and goodwill.

There's an old Arabian proverb: "All things come to him who waits." Apparently it was taken to heart by these men who had worked toward the pinnacle in their various industries.

Perhaps the quality that stood out most about each of these men was the *determination* they exhibited in their lives. They *knew* what they wanted to do, and they were steadfast in their determination to do it regardless of sicknesses, impediments, "general conditions" or the discouragement of others. All of these men were *optimists*, in the sense that they felt they could do what they had set their hearts on doing, in spite of roadblocks that might discourage or deter others.

Ernest E. Norris, as a boy in Illinois, wanted to be a telegraph operator. But jobs were scarce back then. He hung around a telegraph office and learned the Morse code by watching the operator. One day, he read about the death of an operator in a town some distance away. He immediately wrote for the job and got it. Later he went to work for the Southern Railway in a menial capacity. Eventually, he became its president.

James H. Rand invented a visible index, in which he had great faith. His father, who was already in the office machine business, didn't think much of it. So young Rand formed his own company, to compete with his father whom not too many years later, he was able to buy out. Later he formed the giant Remington Rand Company.

If asked to isolate the *one* quality that set all these men apart from their less-successful colleagues, I would have to use one word—*determination.* Cato the Elder used to rise regularly in the Roman Senate to declare: "Carthage must be destroyed." Eventually, as we know, Carthage was destroyed.

The lives of all the fifty foremost convinced me that determination to get to the top—to be successful in every good way—was the prime reason they could attain their goals. In fulfilling this determination they had to exercise all their skills and develop all their good qualities, constantly sharpening these through use and new knowledge.

The inflexible will to succeed enabled them to do it.

EDDIE RICKENBACKER—
A LESSON IN POSITIVE FAITH

by WILLIAM L. ROPER

"Opportunity is very much like a radio signal—unless your receiver is tuned to it you may never contact it. Often it is not repeated. Today you must be on the beam—ready to grasp your chance."

Captain Edward Vernon (Eddie) Rickenbacker, famous air-combat ace of World War I and now chairman of the Board of Directors of Eastern Air Lines, Incorporated, gives this advice to America's ambitious youngsters. But his message is not for the young alone.

Political demagoguery, communism and man's passion to get something for nothing, he warned, form a deadly combination that threatens the future of free enterprise.

"I have no time or patience for those who come to this land of ours to take advantage of our opportunities and then to stab us in the back, nor do I have patience for the fellow travelers," he said.

Declaring that freedom of opportunity was the greatest freedom in America, he said:

"Without that freedom, you would not have the freedom to succeed. Too many people today are looking for the fifth freedom—freedom from work. 'Security' is the most overworked word in the dictionary today."

Certainly Eddie Rickenbacker never asked for security. All he asked was a chance. He never asked for a paternalistic government to protect him from the cradle to the grave. He was willing to work for what he got, and to fight for what he believed.

Therefore, it is logical that he should become a symbol, an outstanding champion of the American way of life, his life an inspiration for the ambitious.

Born in Columbus, Ohio, on Oct. 8, 1890, the third of eight children, Eddie got his first job when he was eleven. The sudden death of his father had made it necessary for him to leave school and go to work to help support his widowed mother and family. His first job was in a glass factory: his salary, $3.50 a week. Later he switched to a machine shop. And when he was four-teen, he got a job in Evan's Garage in Columbus at $4.50 a week, because he was fascinated by automobiles.

In 1905 while working in the garage, Eddie got the idea of supplementing his meager schooling with a correspondence home study course. His mother, always wise and sympathetic, approved. Night after night, Eddie studied earnestly by the light of a kerosene lamp, his lessons spread out on the kitchen table.

There, in those lessons, he found the key to advancement. Coupled with his natural mechanical ability, they equipped him for his next big opportunity—a job in the Frayer-Miller Automobile Company of Columbus.

One spring day, Eddie walked into the Frayer-Miller plant. For some time he stood silently watching Lee Frayer, the plant organizer and head mechanic. Frayer was working on an auto-mobile ignition system. Finally he glanced up and frowned. "Well, boy" he growled, "what do you want?"

"Just thought I'd tell you I'm coming to work here tomorrow morning," Eddie said, looking Frayer squarely in the eye.

Frayer straightened. He studied the tall boy with a puzzled frown. "Oh, you are, are you? Who hired you?"

Eddie smiled. "Nobody yet, but I'll be on the job here in the morning. If I'm not worth anything, you can fire me."

Frayer shrugged. He returned to his task as the boy strode away.

The following morning Eddie reported for work at the Frayer-Miller plant. He had left a hurried note at Evans's Garage, saying "I've quit." Frayer was not at the plant when Eddie arrived, but the boy did not wait for anyone to tell him what to do. He noticed that the floor of the machine shop was covered with a thick layer of metal shavings and dirt. Eddie got a broom and a shovel and started cleaning the place. He had half of the floor clean when Frayer arrived an hour later. Frayer stopped in the doorway and stared in surprise.

A keen-minded businessman, Frayer realized that Eddie Rickenbacker was no ordinary youngster. Here was a boy who was seeking a career instead of just a weekly pay envelope.

One lunch hour, Frayer observed the boy deeply absorbed in a booklet of some kind. He was curious.

"What you got there?" he inquired.

"A correspondence course lesson in automotive engineering," Eddie said. "It's all about carburetors."

Frayer studied the booklet with interest and asked the slender, brown-eyed boy several questions about the course. A week later he transferred Eddie to the carburetor department.

When Eddie was seventeen, Frayer selected him to become his assistant in designing and building a new type touring car. That was in 1907.

Other promotions came quickly, and it was not long until Eddie was branch manager of the Columbus Buggy Company. In spite of his youth, he was chosen to head a sales staff of six men. To sell cars, he had to demonstrate them. This led him into automobile racing, a field in which he soon distinguished himself.

When the 1913 racing season ended, he had placed first or among the first four in a dozen speed events. During the next two years he won several races and gained a national reputation as a racing driver. His prize winnings for 1915 amounted to $24,000.

In the winter of 1916, Rickenbacker wrote a book on automobile racing. He called it *The Book of Rules.* The volume disclosed that he was not the wild, daredevil driver that the public believed him to be, but careful and methodical.

When the United States declared war on Germany in 1917, Rickenbacker, although nearly twenty-seven, offered to organize a group of American racing drivers into a flying corps for the United States Army, something like France's Lafayette Escadrille.

"You're too old and you don't have a college education," an official of the United States Signal Corps explained in turning down Rickenbacker's offer.

Undaunted in his determination to serve in France, Rickenbacker became a chauffeur for the staff of General John J. Pershing. He sailed for France with the first contingent of the A.E.F. Upon arriving in Paris, they were given a wild, joyous reception. Like the other Americans, Eddie was thrilled. But he was not satisfied. He wanted to do something more worthwhile than drive a car, even for the General's staff. He wanted to take part in the air battles that were becoming an increasingly important factor in the war.

He was driving one of General Pershing's staff officers, Major Dodd, over a muddy road near Verdun, when a chance meeting brought him a step nearer his dream. Stalled beside the road was a big twin-six Packard. A sergeant with an oil-grimed face was working under the car's raised hood.

Major Dodd ordered Rickenbacker to see if he could help. One peek at the grimy carburetor suggested the possible trouble to Eddie's trained eye. The carburetor needed cleaning. Quickly he set to work taking it apart and cleaning the carburetor's flow chamber which had become clogged with water and dirt. In a short time, he had the engine purring smoothly.

Colonel William L. (Billy) Mitchell, commander of the American air units in France, who had been waiting while the men worked on his car, flashed a grateful smile at Rickenbacker.

"Say, Sergeant," he said, "it's lucky you came along. You seem to know something about automobile engines."

Dodd grinned, "He should, Colonel. That's Eddie Rickenbacker, the famous racing driver. I'm lucky to have him as my driver."

"You mean you were lucky," replied Mitchell. "Since I outrank you, Major, I'm going to trade drivers with you right now. From now on, Sergeant Rickenbacker is going to be my driver."

Rickenbacker was pleased with his new chauffeuring assignment. Not only did it mean seeing more action, but he liked Colonel Mitchell and his new job brought him in close association with the air force commander. It gave him an opportunity to plead his case.

But when he first told Mitchell of his dream of becoming a

fighting pilot, the Colonel discouraged him.

"You're over the age limit and you don't have the necessary education," Mitchell explained.

Several weeks passed before a burned-out ball-bearing in the Colonel's car gave Rickenbacker a chance to prove how resourceful and expert he was. None of the French garages in Vendôme, where they happened to be, had the kind of bearing needed. So the ingenious Rickenbacker borrowed some Babbitt metal and a blowtorch, and made one. That performance convinced Mitchell that Rickenbacker was no ordinary mechanic—and that he would make a wonderful aviation engineer.

Soon afterwards, he selected Rickenbacker to be an engineering officer for a flying school being set up at Issoudun to train American flyers. Commissioned a second lieutenant in August, 1917, the former racer was sent to Tours for his first air training. Early in 1918, he was flying a combat plane at the front.

Rickenbacker soon was the ace of the American air arm. When the war ended with the signing of the Armistice on November 11, 1918, he had shot down twenty-two German planes and four observation balloons. From September 24 to the end of the war, he commanded the 91st Pursuit Squadron.

Time after time, the Germans sent aloft their most prized aces to get Rickenbacker, but the American ace returned, frequently with a bullet-riddled plane.

Returning to the United States at the end of the war, he was a national hero.

Rickenbacker founded the Rickenbacker Car Company in 1921. After several business adventures, some successful and some not, he raised $3,500,000 in 1938 for the purchase of Eastern Air Lines. Eventually he became president, general manager and director of the company.

During World War II he conducted special missions to Iceland and England, and did reconnaissance for the United States in the South Pacific.

When Rickenbacker and a crew of U.S. airmen, flying a government mission, were forced down in the South Pacific in October 1942, they drifted helplessly for twenty-three days on a rubber raft.

Out there on the vast Pacific, blistered by the tropical sun and near death from hunger and thirst, one man became delirious and slipped from the raft. Others lay prone, almost resigned to never seeing home again, as hungry sharks snapped at them and the blazing sun burned their flesh.

Eddie Rickenbacker bowed his head and prayed.

Then a miracle happened! A seagull came screeching down as from nowhere and perched on Rickenbacker's head. Rickenbacker seized the bird and twisted its neck. This bird became food to revive the men on the raft.

Interviewed at her home in Beverly Hills, while the world anxiously awaited news of the missing men, Eddie Rickenbacker's mother said: "Eddie will come back. He is the luckiest man in the world."

Yes, Eddie came back. Lucky he was, but he had something in addition to luck. He had courage, determination and a will to live, along with an enormous amount of self-reliance.

Ralph Waldo Emerson once wrote an essay on self-reliance, and Eddie Rickenbacker has given the world a living demonstration of it. Without a positive self-faith, he could never have become the American air ace of World War I or accomplished the many other amazing deeds of his career.

"Keep plugging and learning," he advised a group of boys. "Anyone who has the desire and determination to forge ahead cannot help but be successful."

This is the kind of coaching America needs, if we are to meet the challenge of Karl Marx and the faceless robots who march to his credo.

ART LINKLETTER—HIS HAPPINESS IS COMPLETE AT CHRISTMAS

by ADINE TRAVIS LOUGH

Somehow, memories of our childhood Christmases always remain with us. Each year, in brief flashes of memory, we recall scenes of happiness—and sadness—that have been buried from youth, in our subconscious mind.

Art Linkletter has many such memories.

"We were very poor when I was a child," he says. "I suppose I was ten years old before I discovered that not all people got their Christmas dinners in baskets. I worked as an errand boy, swept out stores, picked fruit and sold it door-to-door in order to rustle up a few dollars to buy Christmas gifts for my mother and Dad. But I like to think those gifts were truly representative of the spirit of Christmas. It wasn't their cost that mattered. They were earned by the sweat of my brow and given with love from my heart."

Poverty wasn't the only major obstacle he hurdled in his youth. By accident, as a youngster he discovered that Mary and John Linkletter, the only parents he had ever known, were not his real parents at all. Born Gordon Arthur Kelly, he was given up by his natural parents when he was only a few weeks old. While never denying that the discovery was a cruelly painful one, Linkletter, as a youngster, quite typically put it to work on his own behalf. He immediately transcended the material poverty of the Linkletter home and dreamed of the day when his real father, rich and handsome, would come for him in a big car and drive off to his real home—a mansion on the hill.

"I played this little game of make-believe to see me through the patched shirts and underwear I put on every day," Linkletter said. "I'm only grateful that Father Linkletter, who gave me everything he could, was not aware of it."

John Linkletter was fifty-one years old when he and his wife Mary went to the adoption agency in Moose Jaw, Saskatchewan, for their new son. John's right leg had been amputated after a boyhood accident, and he wore a wooden leg and walked with a cane. Later, he liked to be called the Reverend John Linkletter, although he had never been ordained. He had no church of his own but he was an intensely religious man and he took on Satan in no uncertain terms. He was violently opposed to movies, card-playing, and liquor.

"I remember when I was signed to emcee a show sponsored by a wine company back in 1939," Art Linkletter smiled. "I was afraid Father would explode. Instead, he reminded me of a verse in the Bible which says, 'Drink no longer water but use a little wine for thy stomach's sake and thine own infirmities.'

"And then he added, 'And whenever you can, Artie, give the Lord a little plug.'"

Linkletter speaks of his foster parents with great warmth and affection. Quite obviously the solidity of his own character was carved out of the teachings of these two good people who made him their son.

"But you learn all the way up," Linkletter continued. "I remember when I was a newcomer to Hollywood and was invited to join some truly big stars in a Community Chest benefit show. The theater in Beverly Hills held three thousand seats and I was told it was a once-in-a-lifetime opportunity for a young performer.

"At showtime only fourteen people had appeared. I stood listlessly on stage and decided the whole thing wasn't worth the effort. I got off as fast as I got on.

"Then Jack Benny went on stage for his act. For 35 minutes he entertained these fourteen people as if they were fourteen thousand. I got the message that Benny spelled out for me. As long as even one person comes to see you perform, you owe him the best you can give him. I hope I've done that ever since."

The millions of people who have tuned into "House Party" on CBS for twenty years and "People are Funny" over NBC for twenty-one years are dedicated testimonials to Linkletter and his performance on the air.

"My wife Lois and I have received hundreds of gifts from faithful friends all over the country," Linkletter said gratefully. "We've had giant watermelons from Texas and a barrel of lobsters from Maine. The Los Angeles zoo now houses a baby elephant that was shipped to me from India, and Gene Autry inherited a live bull another friend sent me. We've had cookies and cakes by the carload, argyle socks, turtles and whale blubber. I've even had a dahlia named after me."

Linkletter's genuine interest in people draws audiences to him like a magnet. When people talk to him, he really listens— a trait conspicuously absent in many people who live far less busy lives than his own. His ability to put himself in the other fellow's shoes and to see things from another person's point of view have been responsible in no small part for his success. When you are liked, it's easy to like back. And Linkletter's empathy with the public has gone on for a great many years.

He is a strong believer in family, and happily spends every available free moment with his own. Married for 26 years to Lois Foerster, he has five children, and his grandchildren are a never-failing source of delight to him.

"Children are pretty remarkable people," he grins. "I think the reason 'The Kids' have been such a big hit on 'House Party' for so long is answerable in one word—suspense! You never know what they are going to say but you may be sure it will be said in a refreshingly honest sort of way.

"Besides, children are an adult's link with the long ago. Their unguarded innocence can magically carry you back through the years to your own childhood. And their logic is hard to argue with.

"Take the boy who insisted he had been outside playing ball with God. 'That's ridiculous,' his mother said. 'How could you possibly do that?' 'Well,' said the child, 'I throw the ball up in the air and God throws it back to me!'

"Or the young fellow who delivered this sermon. 'God invented the world and food and spiders and houses and every-thing.' 'Wait a minute,' I asked. 'What if we had no God?' The child looked at me for a moment and then murmured, 'We'd be in a mess.'

"Perhaps it wouldn't hurt any of us to play a little more ball with God or to appreciate His existence," Linkletter smiled. "It might make 'Peace on earth, good will to men' a daily rather than an annual philosophy."

This Christmas, as in the past, will be a family day for the Linkletters, brightened by the love and laughter of their grand-children.

But the true meaning of the day will still permeate the family gathering.

"A few years ago we spend Christmas Eve in the grotto of the Nativity in Bethlehem. A fourteen-pointed silver star glowed warmly over the spot where Christ was born.

"Later, we watched while Christian Arabs from Israel and Jordon clung to each other in joyful reunion, while hardened soldiers from the borders of No-man's land on both sides watched with tears in their eyes.

"So to me," Art Linkletter said, "Christmas is a day of new birth and of new hope for a future that can be lived in love and peace."

DAVID SARNOFF—
HE CHANGED YOUR LIFE

by PAUL MOLLOY

Were Horatio Alger alive today he would begin one of his success stories with every cliché in the book of self-made men:

The boy would be the bewildered son of hopelessly poor immigrants struggling on New York's steamy East Side. The father would die young and the boy would sell newspapers to support his widowed mother. In time he would play a heroic role in a catastrophe, probably a major sea disaster. He would fight life's fearful odds—as one of Alger's titles puts it—and once they were conquered, the President of the United States would call on him for help.

Finally, he would wind up lording an empire he once served as a humble errand boy.

And that would be the story of David Sarnoff—inventor, brigadier general, industrial statesman, head of the worldwide Radio Corporation of America, first to foresee and develop radio as home entertainment, founder of the powerful National Broadcasting Company, and crusader for color television in every American home.

And, in the true Alger tradition, it all started with a happy accident.

Sarnoff came to America at the age of nine from an obscure mudflat in the Russian province of Minsk.

Overwork sidelined his father, who was a painter, and young David sold papers on the streets until he saved enough to establish a newsstand in the rough, tough Hell's Kitchen section of New York. This wasn't sufficient to support the family (two younger brothers) so he sang in a synagogue choir at night—until puberty caught up with his soprano voice. When David was fifteen, his father died and David decided he would need a regular income.

He had already started with newspapers, so why not a newspaper career? David struck out for the old *New York Herald*, walked through the first door that looked interesting, and snapped up a $5-a-week messenger job.

The flustered boy hadn't noticed the sign on the door: Commercial Cable Company.

Once in, he was promptly seduced by the mystery and nervous music of the telegraph key. His first savings went toward a key and code book and, utterly captivated by this new magic and its potential, he devoted all of his spare time to the practice of Morse code. His interest and ambition were so genuine that friendly operators on occasions would give him a turn at the live key.

That was all Sarnoff needed. Off he scurried to the Marconi Wireless Company of America: Could they use an assistant telegrapher? They couldn't but they needed an office boy at $5.50 a week. Sarnoff grabbed it, not because of the extra half-dollar a week, but because he'd have a chance to see the celebrated Guglielmo Marconi.

This was 1906. One day Marconi the genius and the office boy Sarnoff would together develop the power of the electron and become bosom friends.

First, though, Sarnoff had achieved his preliminary goal—to become a telegrapher. More time and money went into books and studies and, at seventeen, he made it. He was assigned to a lonely Marconi wireless station on Nantucket Island. Salary: $70 a month, $40 of which went to his mother. The station was a decrepit place but it was well stocked with technical books. Sarnoff all but memorized them and as his knowledge and thirst for knowledge increased, he was promoted to Marconi's new station atop the Wanamaker store in central Manhattan.

There, on the night of April 14, 1912, he caught a fatal SOS from a ship far out at sea. The message signed off: "SS Titanic."

For seventy-two hours Sarnoff stayed with his key until he had reported the name of the last survivor to a shocked nation.

The three-day marathon caught the public imagination, wireless ceased being a freak, won a new name (radio) and was on its way.

So was Sarnoff.

It's easy to say that Sarnoff happened to be at the right place at the right time. This is only partly true. Sarnoff had to be ready and equipped to be at the right place at the right time.

Five years later (1917) Sarnoff was commercial manager of American Marconi Company, astounded that his superiors did not yet recognize that radio could benefit and help the individual, in the privacy of the home, with "a little box and amplifying tubes." The commercial aspects were almost incredible. He fired memos unceasingly, outlining his plans and even accurately predicting the number of sets that could be sold in the formative years.

Nobody paid much attention at the time, but World War I was to finally prove the value of radio communications. After the war, the U.S. government moved to break the foreign control (mostly British) of the Marconi firm, and the result in 1919 was an all-American company—RCA—formed with American capital by U.S. industrialists. Sarnoff handled much of the business transaction (at the request of the Navy's assistant secretary, Franklin Delano Roosevelt) and became its general manager.

In 1930, at the age of thirty-nine, Sarnoff became president of RCA.

Between 1919 and then, however, Sarnoff had pushed for his dream. He needled the company into investing $2,000 in his "little box"; coaxed them into believing in his dream of short wave radio; argued that not only would radio *not* kill the phonograph but that the two would "live under one roof" (the same cabinet); accurately forecast two-way radio for cars and the walkie-talkie; foresaw the use of electric sockets for radio juice (eliminating storage batteries) and, in 1927, described "a radio-controlled tank of the future, without human pilotage, being driven toward the enemy's lines" (the guided missile).

A prominent engineer of that day shook his head and said: "Wireless never caught up with Sarnoff." Not long ago Sarnoff offered his own explanation: "I have learned from long experience to have more faith in the scientist than he has in himself."

Much of his uncanny forethought is history: As early as 1923 he warned of chaos in the air without policing, and recommended government regulation of broadcasting channels. He correctly estimated that radio services could be paid for by the sales of sets and advertising.

He was working with television in 1923 ("It will come to pass," he said) and later RCA was to pour $50 million into TV research, reportedly the largest such single investment. His theory: "Would you rather be deaf or blind? Radio can hear, it will remain blind until television is a fact."

Today, RCA is the world's largest all-electronic company and has been doing one billion dollars worth of business annually since 1955.

He and his company have been at the government's service in peace and in war because, as he explains: "I shall never be out of debt to America. Nothing I have done would have been possible except in the American climate of freedom."

What sort of man, in private life, is this scientific genius?

Mrs. Sarnoff, a Parisian he married in 1917, says this of him: "He is convinced absolutely that there is a Supreme Force over the universe. The closer he has come to the electron and the atom, the more he has come to see that there is order and beauty in the universe and a force behind everything. He has seen the world more clearly than other men may have, perhaps, and is more aware how miraculous it is."

A wealthy man, Sarnoff abhors the practice of tipping. Not because he likes to hang onto money, but because it embarrasses him that one human being should give another small change for a small service. He tips the proper people annually.

Like many men, he tends to become overweight but his wife keeps him in check. He doesn't care for sports but once was talked into taking up horseback riding in Central Park. In the morning he would rise, peek out of the window and, if it were raining, exclaim: "Thank goodness, I don't have to ride today!" To handle his appetite, Mrs. Sarnoff always keeps a box of candies in her purse for him. Says she: "You see, even a genius has the most charmingly childlike traits."

Sarnoff likes to have a cigar and read the morning papers without interruption, so he and his wife have breakfast in separate rooms. He loves gadgets and enjoys relaxing in a barber's chair—so his wife has installed such a chair, with the works, in their big New York home as well as another one in their Washington apartment.

Sarnoff detests interruptions because they offend his sense of orderly thinking and, when in the company of bores, he gives a magnificent impression of being an avid listener. Actually he has already shifted mental gears and directed his mind to technical things that interest and challenge him. But he still gives the appearance of courteous absorption.

Sarnoff has two mottoes. One is: *Think before you talk.* This indicates that, while he has rushed through life doing many things while others plod along contentedly, he cannot be rushed on problems related to his work and interest.

The other motto is: *The soup never has to be eaten as hot as it is served.* This is his answer when associates show alarm or panic.

But the reason behind his startling success was perhaps best illustrated late in 1951 when he celebrated his forty-fifth year in radio. He spoke of the fiftieth year achievements of radio and electronics and said they would be eclipsed within the next decade. Then he added:

"Anything that the human mind can conceive can be produced ultimately."

BOB CUMMINGS—"LIVE IN A DREAM FULFILLED"

by ADINE TRAVIS LOUGH

Delivered at birth by his doctor father, married by his minister mother, and named in part after Orville Wright, his father's close friend, Charles Clarence Robert Orville Cummings, Jr., could not do anything but aim for the spotlight, it seems.

Bob Cumming's philosophy for success was generated by a father who firmly believed that anyone could accomplish anything he wanted *if he would live, think, talk, act, eat and sleep as if his goal had already been achieved.*

"Dad called it 'living in a dream fulfilled' " Bob smiled. "And that was years before Rogers and Hammerstein wrote 'If you ain't got a dream, how you gonna make a dream come true?'

"I was subjected to Dad's philosophy meal after meal, day after day, and year after year," Cummings continued. "It made for pretty humdrum listening until one day, when I needed it most, the meaning of what he was saying exploded in my mind. It's worked for me in a variety of ways ever since."

Certainly, Bob's accomplishments prove that he has had something big going for him. Few men, even those blessed with his talents, have sustained such great success for so long a time in such a variety of fields.

He is a commercial instrument pilot and holds the first flight instructor's rating ever issued. During the war, he turned out over seventy combat flyers. Flying to him is not a sport, it is a way of life and he does it professionally.

He played straight man to Milton Berle in vaudeville and did literally hundreds of radio shows in New York. He is a graduate of the Ziegfeld follies and Earl Carroll Vanities.

He has starred in over a hundred movies. While he is perhaps best known for his comedy roles, he has played dramatic parts in such films as *Dial 'M' for Murder, The Carpetbaggers* and *Stagecoach* with equal skill and facility. In fact he received television's highest award for his dramatic role in *Twelve Angry Men.*

He has been the star of four network television series. In his *Bob Cummings Show,* he not only financed the production but also starred in all of the episodes for over five years, contributed to the writing of some, directed most, played "Grandpa" in many and did all of his own "Grandpa's" flying. Quite a career in itself for any individual.

But perhaps Bob Cummings's greatest achievement is his status as a human being. His life revolves around his wife Mary and his five youngsters—Robert, Melinda, Patricia, Laurel Ann, and Tony. Where Bob goes, they go. Earlier this year, the whole family accompanied him to England where he made a movie called *Promise Her Anything.* Recently, they flew with him in his plane "The Wayward Stork" on his try-out tour of a play. "When my family is with me," Bob smiles, "I don't really feel I'm away from home." He loathes the phoney and somehow manages to stay the same whether he's out with old friends such as Art Linkletter, Conrad Hilton, Henry Kaiser or talking to a fan. "They're all important to me." Many stars make this kind of statement. With Bob, you know it's true.

This doesn't keep him from being ridiculed by some for his interest in proper diet and food supplements. ("Though if I'd taken as many pills as I've been accused of, I wouldn't have had time to do anything else in my entire lifetime," he says.) To understand this side of him, it is necessary to go back to his own "Life with Father."

Charles Cummings, Sr., prepared himself for the ministry, but he was possessed by the idea that *Man is what he eats and thinks,* and he became a doctor, instead. He was convinced, even before the turn of the century, that man's ideal diet should be balanced about 90 per cent in favor of a complete protein diet. He considered the insufficiencies of civilized man's diet shocking, and set about creating a way to replace and/or supplement these deficiencies.

As Bob says, "I was reared on some of the world's screwiest tasting concoctions. But, looking back, Dad's opinions on nutrition were the forerunner of what is medically accepted as sound today."

Dr. Cummings, for all of his interest in nutrition, did not forsake the ministry. He married it. Bob's mother was known to the citizens of Joplin, Missouri as Mrs. Reverend Doctor Cummings, an ordained minister. In fact, when Bob married Mary Elliot Daniels of Gaffney, South Carolina, his mother performed the ceremony.

To go back a bit, when Bob was born, his father delivered him. "There are those who put this admittedly thrifty procedure down to my Scottish ancestry," Bob grins. "If so, they must certainly have enjoyed the selection I made for our first-born's godfather. The man who held Robert Richard in his arms at the christening was no less than Jack Benny!"

His father's friendship with Orville Wright had strange beginnings. Dr. Cummings was hurriedly summoned one evening to the Southern Pacific depot grounds in Joplin, where a small, dilapidated circus tent was pitched. Inside, Orville Wright was writhing with ptomaine poisoning. Outside, he and his brother Wilbur had roped off their "crackpot invention" on display for the people to see. The ropes were totally unnecessary as no one ventured near. Orville Wright was cured of his malady in a matter of hours, but his friendship with Bob's father endured throughout their lives.

Wright's idealistic phrases, "America will soon become a grasshopper nation," "Airplanes will elevate civilization from the mud of ignorance to the clean air of knowledge," and "Every town and farm will one day own its own airdrome" were laughed at by most but not by Dr. Cummings. The one-hundred-acre Joplin, Missouri, airdrome (donated by one of the doctor's patients, August Schiffendecker) was dedicated the year after Bob was born, and the three Cummings attended the dedication. In fact, Dr. Cummings presided and his wife said an early day "sky-pilot" prayer. On the same ground in 1927, Bob soloed in a Travelair biplane designed by Lloyd Stearman and Walter Beech. That plane, affectionately known as "old number one," is the plane "Grandpa" flew in *The Bob Cummings Show.*

Bob's flying made him one of the most unusual fund raisers in Hollywood. "Winning" Cummings as a door prize means that from 5 to 245 people per charity event get free rides in Bob's own Piper Aztec twin-engined plane, with the star himself piloting them.

Asked why he does it, Cummings, who has won innumerable awards for his contribution to the science, art and popularization of aviation, says simply: "Well, I'm not an entertainer in the sense that such greats as Danny Kaye and Jack Benny are. I'm not a singer like Sinatra or Dean Martin. So when I'm asked to appear at a charity event, I tell them that I'll do what I do best—fly my plane for them.

"You'd be amazed to learn the high percentage of Americans who have never flown . . . never even set foot in a plane. Only about 12 per cent of the U.S. population has ever flown. In Europe, more than 20 per cent fly regularly, if only on a vacation.

"But at these charity affairs, people who could afford to fly but who haven't either out of apathy or a baseless fear, rush to try to win the prize flights. They seem to like the idea."

That's putting it mildly. Recently, the United Way committee was having a hard time getting enough attendance to fill one dining room at their Bel-Air Hotel luncheon meeting. Then they announced that a flight with Cummings would be the door prize. Immediately they were faced with the dilemma of either moving the event to a larger place or of using two dining rooms at the hotel.

There's only one drawback to Bob's door-prize flights for charity. Bob's promise to fly the winners is always fulfilled on the following weekend, when they meet him at the Santa Monica Airport. This means precious time away from his family. But Cummings solved that problem his own way. He takes fewer passengers on each ride, but now his children take turns accompanying him and his passengers on each flight.

If anyone doubts the potency of Dr. Cummings's philosophy for success, they have only to look to his son. "Living in a dream fulfilled" has worked out mighty well for Charles Clarence Robert Orville Cummings, Jr.

STEVE McQUEEN—
"ALWAYS BE YOURSELF"

by WILLIAM L. ROPER

Dare to be an individual!

There, in that one line, you have the key to the noncon-formist thinking that has made Steve McQueen, one-time juvenile delinquent, an outstanding film and television star. Now at thirty-six, he is earning $500,000 a year. And a few years ago, *Time* Magazine nominated him the most logical successor of John Wayne, top Hollywood Western actor.

In thinking and working his way out of what once looked like a dead-end street, the boyish-faced McQueen has pointed up certain lessons in self-improvement which should inspire and help young and old alike. His story is particularly inspiring for those at the bottom of the ladder.

For not so many years ago, Terrence Stephen McQueen was down there himself. His problems began early in life. Not long after his birth in Indianapolis, Indiana, on March 24, 1930, his parents were divorced. He never knew his father, who was killed while flying in China for Chennault's Raiders. For a few years he and his mother lived with her uncle on a farm in Slater, Missouri. But when Steve was six, his mother remarried. That was the beginning of new trouble. To quote McQueen: "I loved my mother, but my stepfather was something else again."

Feeling frustrated and unloved, he began running with a wild gang of youthful delinquents when his mother and stepfa-ther moved to California. At fourteen, he had become such a problem child that his parents decided he should be placed in a correctional institution. So they sent him to the California

Junior Republic, a privately operated rehabilitation school for wayward boys at Chino, California.

Although Steve admits he was miserable during his first months at the school, he gives the school counselors credit for calming him down and talking some sense into him during a particularly trying period of his youth.

"I went to school in the morning and in the afternoon worked in the laundry," he recalls. "That laundry bugged me, and after about three months of it, I took off."

His attempted runaway, however, was unsuccessful. He had gone only a few miles when police captured him and returned him to the Junior Republic. Upon his return, he expected a severe paddling. But instead, a staff member put his arm around Steve's shoulders and talked to him like an older brother.

"He began to get through to me," Steve said. From that time on, Steve behaved himself and began taking a new interest in his studies.

Meanwhile, his stepfather died and his mother moved to New York. She sent for Steve. After a brief stay with his mother, he shipped out as an ordinary seaman on a tanker bound for the West Indies. Then after more adventures as a laborer in the Texas oil fields and a tree topper in Canada, he enlisted in the Marine Corps.

After doing his hitch in the Marines, which included cold-weather amphibious maneuvers in Labrador, he was discharged at Camp Lejeune, North Carolina, in April of 1950. His military pay did not last long. Once more he was adrift without a job. He went to New York, rented a cold-water flat in Greenwich Village for nineteen dollars a month. There he tried selling encyclopedias and earning a precarious living by various part-time jobs.

The hardships that he encountered in these unprofitable ventures knocked into Steve's head what counselors at the Junior Republic and other adults had been trying unsuccessfully to tell him for years: that it pays to learn a craft; that a man without a craft, skill or a profession has a hard time in today's world. A girl he met in Greenwich Village also helped him to get started on the right track.

"You ought to try acting," she said. She suggested he go to

see Sanford Meisner, director of the Neighborhood Playhouse.

Meisner was impressed with the youthful McQueen. At least the kid was different. He was an individual, not trying to imitate some celebrity.

"Yes, I think it was his original personality," Meisner said later. "He insisted on being himself."

McQueen studied at the Playhouse for two years. A G.I. Bill of Rights scholarship helped to finance his training. How important is such training? He said:

"Like any profession, it is important for an actor—whether he is interested in Westerns, musicals or drama—to learn his craft. This requires time and effort. The boy or girl interested in an acting career should study with a competent coach or dramatic school to obtain the background that is essential. Most actors put in at least five years of training before they become an 'overnight success.' Actually, there is no such thing as an 'overnight success.' I've been in the business since 1953. With Westerns in mind, specifically, it is helpful if the actor is knowledgeable of the tools of the trade. For instance, he must know how to ride and handle a gun. First and foremost, though, it is important to have a good background and basic knowledge of the craft."

In other words, you have to be an actor—and that is much more important than being quick on the draw or knowing how to handle a cow pony.

While attending Manhattan's Neighborhood Playhouse, Steve won a scholarship to the Herbert Berghof Studio, and later received further training at the Actor's Studio in New York. His career really began when he replaced Ben Gazzara in Broadway's *Hatful of Rain* in 1956. He married Neile Adams, a dancer-singer in *Pajama Game,* that year. Today they live in a beautiful mountain-top home in Hollywood and have two children.

Although he is best know as the reckless bounty hunter in the CBS television series, "Wanted—Dead or Alive," he has played important roles in "Never So Few," "The Magnificent Seven," "Hell Is for Heroes," "Great Escape," "Love with the Proper Stranger," "Soldier in the Rain," "The Traveling Lady" and "The Cincinnati Kid."

Talking with him, you soon discover that the real Steve

McQueen is much more than the 174-pound, nearly six-foot maverick you have admired on the screen. He is also a philosopher and a shrewd businessman.

"Every bit of money I make I am investing in things that will make it secure for my wife and family," he said.

With a shy smile, he explained that he believed he had matured quite a bit since the wild adventurous days of his youth, and that he was devoted to his craft.

"I believe I'm still learning," he added. "I love my craft. I swing with what I'm doing. When acting ceases to be fun, that's the time to give it up. I enjoy acting. I truly like my work. But the public is often unaware that acting is also hard work. Most days I'm up at 5:00 A.M. to be on the set by 6:30 for make-up and wardrobe assignments. Often I don't get home till 7:30 in the evening or later. Nights when I work out at the gym, and I try to do this three times a week to keep in shape, I may not get home until 10:00 P.M. With this kind of schedule, you have to like what you're doing."

McQueen makes no claim of having any secret formula for success, but he believes he has learned a few of the rules in the school of hard knocks.

Rule one: he says, is to be yourself—dare to be an individual—don't try to copy someone else's style.

Rule two: study and work to improve yourself in your chosen craft.

Rule three: have a positive mental attitude and the courage to try. In other words, dare to take a chance.

Those who think he is now on top because of some miraculous luck forget the long hours of hard work that he spent in preparation for his career, he points out.

"Hard work is essential to any lasting success," he adds. "Don't let work bug you."

RUDY VALLEE—
THE FEELING OF SUCCESS

by RUDY VALLEE
as told to Larston D. Farrar

Numerous persons have asked me the same question in the past few years. With a few minor variations in wording, it always boils down to this: "Rudy, how does it feel to have made a successful comeback at the age of sixty?"

My reply—and I've reached a point beyond irritation and can only be amused—is, "How can I make a comeback when I've never been away?"

As a mater of fact, during the years when I was out of the national limelight—from about 1950, when my nationwide radio show went off the air, until I bounced back in 1962 as co-star in the Broadway play "How to Succeed in Business Without Really Trying"—I was still very much in touch with the public.

I appeared in hundreds of supper clubs and night spots from coast to coast, drawing good crowds and earning sums which, by any standard, would be counted as "handsome" by the average man.

My wife and I traveled together to many engagements, and we caught new glimpses of a growing, changing, kaleidoscopic, expanding nation at work and at play. I believe that those years were as productive and happy for me and to me as the years when I starred weekly in my own radio show with listeners by the millions. And those years were as fruitful as the more recent period when I have co-starred in a Broadway hit show.

To me, the capacity to earn money has never been a measurement of success. It is my belief that a person must develop a philosophy early in life which permits him to have as much pleasure, enjoyment and satisfaction *now* as is possible without injuring himself or others. Money can help to do this, but it is not and must not become the sole aim of a person's existence. We all know what happened to King Midas.

Back in the little town in Maine where my father was proprietor of a drugstore, I learned that success must be something that a person *feels*. It is in his own head and heart. I also learned that success, both figuratively and literally, is in each person's hands—what he does with the time and tools available to him each day.

Success is a subjective concept, so it must necessarily be in our heads. To use an old phrase, "One man's meat is another man's poison." To a man who has goals of great political power, there is no feeling of being successful unless he wins the race for Governor, for Senator, for President, or whatever office he seeks. Another person whose goal is to be head bookkeeper of his company has succeeded when he is promoted to the desired job. He *has* achieved success, the kind he wanted, and no one can take that feeling from him.

My earliest ambition was to become a good saxophonist. In those days, a half century ago, there were relatively few saxophonists in the United States. Only a handful of men were tops with the instrument. I not only idolized them, I wrote fan-letters and mimicked them and strove to learn from them. My burning ambition was to be like them, and as good with the sax as they were. When I could play as well as the top men of those days, I achieved the *feeling* of success.

That feeling has never left me, although in later years I became better known in other fields. My sax was always close at hand, but I realized that it had been a stepping-stone to other goals.

After playing my saxophone in a small theater, I was able to convince my father that I could earn money. He became reconciled to the fact that I would never be a druggist, as he had hoped. But it took me a longer time to realize that big success is preceded by a period of preparation. Writers go through a "gestation" period before a story or a play or book is actually underway. Persons in other fields have similar experiences before developing a complete idea.

Because I had used my head and hands—my talents and my energies—to learn how to achieve in one field, I was able to use the knowledge gained thereby to act, to direct a band, to direct a radio show, to help choose songs and talent for popular appeal and appraisal.

Philosophers have had much to say about personal achievement, but as I have studied their various works, they seem to agree that success is in each man's head and in his own hands.

Alan Seeger, the American poet, asserted: "Success in life means doing that thing which nothing else conceivable seems more noble or satisfying or remunerative." He meant that which paid off in satisfaction and in good feeling as well as in money.

The great German philosopher Nietzsche wrote that "Nothing ever succeeds which exuberant spirits have not helped to produce."

Alexander Smith, the Scottish poet, said: "In the wide area of the world, failure and success are not accidents, as we so frequently suppose, but the strictest justice. If you do your fair day's work, you are certain to get your fair day's wage—in praise or pudding, whichever happens to suit your taste."

And Benjamin Disraeli, English statesman, writer and Prime Minister to Queen Victoria, once said: "The secret of success is constancy to purpose."

Although my rise in radio was called "meteoric," I had prepared myself for big goals by going to college, playing with bands on weekends and by taking part in college activities. Through working, studying, playing and meeting the challenges of young manhood, I learned how things worked in show business. I learned to seek good advice from those best equipped to give it to me. Also I learned that sometimes the best advice given with the best intentions still goes sour. Ultimately, I began to realize that each of us must make his own decisions.

That early practice playing in nightclub bands proved invaluable when I went on the stage as a radio performer at the New York Paramount and the Brooklyn Paramount. This, in turn, prepared me for Hollywood and a movie career that interspersed my radio performances in the 1930s.

The years I was not in the national scene—from 1950 to

1961—were not periods of idleness. I was not "away." I changed my method of serving the public. I was able to be flexible. Those years permitted me to improve my appearance, voice and mannerisms before live audiences in small, intimate nightclubs. Thus, I considered myself better prepared for a new career—a role in "How to Succeed in Business Without Really Trying."

When the play was pronounced a success by the seven key New York critics and assured a long run, the sacrifices, rigorous days and nights of rehearsals, one-night-stands in small cities as a nightclub performer were forgotten. When the crowds began to scramble for seats to this new Broadway play, I knew I was experiencing still another type of achievement and preparing for opportunities the future might offer!

FLORENCE CHADWICK— "WINNERS NEVER QUIT; QUITTERS NEVER WIN"

by HARVEY J. BERMAN

Late in 1952, with television facilities spanning a nation focused on her alone, Florence Chadwick strode into the outgoing tide and began her epic-making swim from Catalina Island to Los Angeles, across a channel noted for its treacherous undertow, its tricky currents and the heavy pull of the tides. Fourteen hours later, she reached the coastline and an estimated 50 million TV onlookers, held by the taut dream of a woman defying the sea, cheered as one.

Not that it was the first time that Florence Chadwick had attempted the seemingly impossible and succeeded. In 1950, for example, she announced that she would venture the grind from cap Gris Nez, France, to St. Margaret's Bay in England.

When informed of the perils she faced, Florence smiled politely, heard the speaker out, and then quietly related how as a girl she had set her mind on a Channel crossing and how she had spent years preparing for it. "Don't ask me how I know I'll make it," she declared, eyes flashing. "I just have known all along that when the right moment came I'd be here and would make it to the other side."

Her firm belief that she would succeed where others had failed was not based on whimsy. Because she had so earnestly longed to swim the strait, she had studied it thoroughly. She had also carefully analyzed the swimming techniques of those who had won out and had accepted their best for her own.

When she finally stepped into the surf and started from the French coast, battling an adverse sea and high winds all the way, her stroke was easy and accurately calculated to bring her to England, and an amazed world prepared to hail the woman who conquered the "Cap Gris Nez death run."

Yet no matter how much the world saw of the swimmer during the next few months, it still could have no real conception of what success really meant to Florence Chadwick, an internationally famous aquatic star who once, however, almost gave up her career in despair.

At the age of six, she had been entered by her father in a San Diego race. The distance was exactly fifty yards, and her parents, who had watched her past performances with undisguised enthusiasm, were certain that their daughter—at home more in the water than on land—would triumph.

However, Florence was the last to reach the finish line. A year later at San Clemente, despite the fact that she had prepared for the event with quiet fury and intensity, she failed again.

It was a bewildered youngster who returned home and unhappily clung to her father. But detective Richard Chadwick knew his daughter better than she knew herself. The water was her life and he had faith in her ability.

"Let's try it together," he told her soon after her fiasco. "Sometimes we tend to forget that a team can accomplish far more than any individual player. Well, now we're a team, you and I. Let's work, plan, and try together—and in the end, we'll win together."

Florence studied and practiced with seemingly endless persistence for the next five years. At the age of eleven she won her first major victory—a six-mile endurance trial.

Excited, at last certain that the motto she believed in, "Winners never quit; quitters never win," would now begin to pay big dividends, Florence Chadwick became totally sea-minded. For hours each day, without exception, and in the winter's chill as well as the summer's heat, she became a familiar sight in the waters around San Diego. Through little advancements in her technique, she gained speed and stamina, as well as the all-important reservoir of self-confidence. And always, when in trouble, she could turn to her father and the "team."

Soon after her fourteenth birthday, she told her father, "I

think I'm ready for a try at the National Backstroke title." He listened, broke into a smile, and asked simply, "Are you sure, Florence? How do you know?" To which his daughter replied, "I know I'm ready because this time I'm sure I'm going to win."

Only one obstacle stood between Florence and a coveted national championship award. That barrier was another equally determined young lady, Eleanor Holm.

Florence never won her cup. In as exciting a race between backstrokers as this nation has ever witnessed, Miss Holm went on to earn national acclaim, while Florence had to content herself with the other titles she had won that year.

At about this time, she began to wonder if a career in the water was meant for her. That doubt was to linger for many years. "Sure," she once told a group of friends, "I can win my share, take long-distance events, and manage to do pretty well all around against competition." But to a girl who wanted to win as badly as Florence Chadwick, being an "also ran" in the big contests wasn't quite good enough.

With the announcement of the upcoming 1936 Olympics, the tryouts claimed her attention. Back to the pool she went, determined to make a "do-or-die" attempt. If she failed, she vowed, she would drop swimming, never to come back to it again.

But when the preliminaries were held to select an American team, the story for Florence was the same. She placed fourth, one rung away from a berth.

"I've had it," the tired star told newspapermen on the after-noon of her defeat.

In the years that followed, she turned to Hollywood, swam through a few movies and married. Her name faded from the American aquatic scene.

Then, after years out of the water, she realized that swim-ming had been her entire life. Somewhere along the way, she had lost sight of the fact that medals weren't everything. "I guess I always understood what I wanted out of life. But that under-standing became clouded, perhaps by a relentless desire to win, to be the best. The real values showed through at last. I decided that most of all, I wanted to swim. If the awards came, so much the better. But to be in the water, from that moment on, became the all-important thing."

In August 1950, Florence freed herself from the long and bitter years of frustration at last when she swam across the choppy English Channel in thirteen hours and twenty minutes.

A year later, she was back at the Channel to swim the more treacherous route—from England to France. People were none too optimistic about her chances. For weeks, English newspapers had reported that in swimming from England to France, she was risking her life to no avail. She would never succeed.

During this period, she said nothing, waiting patiently for the Channel to grow calmer and for the dense haze to lift. Finally, before dawn one morning, she made her bid. Kissing her father farewell, she began a trip that was to make her internationally famous overnight.

Those who witnessed it later reported that her swim was one of the most remarkable attempts ever made by anyone—man or woman—on the difficult strait. But to Florence herself, it was perhaps as close to death as she ever will come in the water again. Only minutes out, she realized full well that her life hung in the balance.

After three hours, agonizing cramps gripped her, first in her legs and then in her stomach. As the day progressed, the fog, instead of clearing, grew thicker. As one onlooker put it, "It was like smothering slowly under a heavy woolen blanket."

In the meantime, aboard the boat escorting her, the swimmer's ailing father took ill suddenly and, to complicate matters, when night fell her guides and she became separated at sea. In London, it was reported that Florence was missing. Emergency auxiliary craft were readied for dispatch.

She looked around her, saw nothing but the sea. As she was to point out later, "There was nothing else to do but go on, so I did."

A short time later her escort boat found her and they continued together.

Sixteen hours later, a dog-tired, dazed Florence Chadwick stumbled onto the French beach. While the crowd roared its approval, she collapsed, and asking only about her father, she permitted the sleep she had fought for two-thirds of a day in the water to claim her. When she was to awake, she was to find that the world had labeled her "the greatest female swimming star of all time."

The fate that she had battled for thirty years had at last turned, and Florence Chadwick—"with God's patient help," as she explained it—had become an unqualified success. "Winners never quit; quitters never win" was the motto she had once adopted. Through the agonizing frustration of repeated failure she had gone on to prove its validity not only to the world, but to a harder-to-please Florence Chadwick.

DAVID JANSSEN—
FUGITIVE FROM FAILURE

by DUANE VALENTRY

What makes the man behind *The Fugitive* run? David Janssen, now a top star because of the popular television series, gives reality to the part because for many years he had been on the run himself—from failure.

"To some people, success produces nothing but the fear of failure," he says. "It can be a curse. I think if you're successful you should at least be able to sit back and enjoy it. Having been broke once, I'm not afraid of being broke again. I won't appreciate it though!"

During his ups and downs, David Janssen once ran up a bill at a restaurant close to one thousand dollars—credit extended because the owner believed in him as much as he believed in himself.

"But there are those who accept generosity and trust and promptly disappear when they're in a position to pay," says a friend. "Not David. The minute he was able to, he started paying on his account. The balance went down—then one day the owner received a check in full."

Today he spends much of his leisure time at this restaurant and is its strongest booster.

"If he likes you, there's nothing he wouldn't do," agrees a friend, composer Peter Rugolo. "And he doesn't forget you."

Peter wrote the music for the *Richard Diamond, Detective* series in which Janssen starred several years ago. When he was offered the current series, David made certain that the musical score of *The Fugitive* was written by Rugolo.

Grateful to those who played a part in his career and who believed in him, he doesn't hesitate to say so. He also generously credits his wife with much of his success since their marriage seven years ago.

"Ours is a great marriage," he says, "and it's all Ellie's doing. She has a sense of humor and she's understanding. Ellie made me more sociable. I never had many friends before our marriage. But I have them now—good friends—and Ellie is responsible. People are drawn to her. Unavoidably, maybe, they are drawn to me, too. I relax more around people now and I don't question their every move. When I do, Ellie ribs the heck out of me and that takes care of that."

As a boy, when his show business mother moved many times and then remarried, there was the need to adjust—to new surroundings, to a stepfather—and he did.

In 1957 when he starred in the *Richard Diamond* series, he thought his fun from failure was at an end and admits he "lived it up."

"I was part playboy and part bum. My life consisted mainly of cashing my pay check and paying off my tailor—and my bar tabs."

But the network dropped his show and he felt the ground go out from under him. So many "Diamond" fans protested, however, that it was resumed. This happened four times and each time the actor had a difficult adjustment to make. But the series lasted four seasons and each time it was renewed his salary went up.

There was something missing, though, in his carefree bachelor existence and he was beginning to realize it. Then he met Ellie Graham, a divorcee with two teen-age daughters, and a solid friendship finally led to marriage and the adjustment of owning his own home for the first time along with assuming the responsibilities of marriage and a family.

"Nothing ever seemed to be a problem with David—either success or the lack of it," says his sister. "He was always able to cope with anything. He tries to work his problems out by himself."

There's no lazy success, no sitting on your laurels and no time to quit educating yourself, in this man's opinion.

"He's an extremely literate man who reads constantly," an associate notes. "In fact, he keeps us abreast of what to read. And his opinions and observations are brilliant."

Words interest him, and he is an enemy of the cliché in any form. But literate as he is, some say he has a deep inferiority complex over his lack of a college education, despite the fact that he signed his first contract, with Universal, when he was twenty-one. Why does he read so much? "I figure when I get older, I'll have something to talk about!"

When Janssen bought a Cadillac, friends say he was afraid it might be a "status image."

"Why do I drive it? Because it's so comfortable and I love it!"

No pretensions here—he makes fun of the movie star image frequently, while appreciating to the full its advantages. Nor does Dr. Richard Kimble's alter ego enjoy talking about himself. He won't do it if he can get out of it.

A lack of order disturbs David Janssen now that he has that security and stability so long missing from his life. Often kidded by friends about it, he hangs up everybody's coat or jacket, with the mumbled excuse: "My nature—very neat."

His own impeccable appearance has become a trademark. "I hardly ever have to clean my clothes because I just don't get them dirty," he shrugs.

He wasn't always that way. "I was very sloppy, from twelve to twenty-two. I used to throw everything around out of defiance for having to be neat." Now he tells daughters Kathy and Diane that it's "better for their mental state to have a neat room."

Dr. Richard Kimble is a kind man who helps people, and viewers trust him. David Janssen sometimes hides behind a façade because he genuinely dislikes sentimentality or a show of emotion, but it doesn't fool those who know him.

"It's not hostility directed toward people," says an actress who works with him, "and not a personal thing. I've *never* heard him speak in a deprecating way of people he's worked with. His cynicism is directed toward restrictions, ways of life, social atmosphere, pretension."

If he does get angry, he doesn't let his anger show, according to his sister, who adores him. "I'm sure there have been several crises in his life, as in everyone's, but David is a very sweet person and he stays that way."

In this modern age, success is still synonymous with hard work, insists Jansen.

"You have no idea how much work goes into an hour show. It's three times harder than doing a half-hour show and that's not faulty arithmetic. We need seven days to complete a show so it takes a lot of time juggling to get haircuts, buy clothes, have a social life of sorts and tell my wife I love her. But sometimes, even when I'm doing those things, my mind is with Dr. Kimble and his problems." Yet he had to be urged to take a two-and-one-half week vacation not long ago.

"It was really my first vacation—I just never had time before, and if I did I was broke. This time I had the money to go and a career to come back to. But I wouldn't want to do that every day—I like to work. The vacation is a reward for the work."

Success is rarely gained without setbacks. David recalls his first big one when he hurt his knee during a pole-vault competition in his senior year of high school. There were athletic scholarships waiting for him at two universities and he had to turn them both down.

There were also disappointments in the acting field which helped make him the man he is today.

"I guess it was being too small or too tall for the part for too many years," he says. Universal dropped him after his return from two bleak years in the Army.

"It was a pretty frustrating time. You're impatient. You feel that if you have talent why don't they see it? Your ego is wounded. But this town is filled with people who were turned down and went on to become great successes.

"Whenever things went wrong, I'd brood for weeks. Then Ellie would say that lots of disappointing things happen for the best and something better will come along, and something always did."

When the staring role in *The Fugitive* was first offered to him, David considered it for some time before accepting.

"I had doubts about the fugitive character—he was mostly negative, always running away. But we found ways to strengthen him."

Today, fascinated with Dr. Kimble, he is glad he owns a part of the show which shows no sign of decreasing in popularity.

"Sometimes I have the nice feeling that each morning several planes take off in all directions carrying prints of *The Fugitive*. It was even showing in Puerto Rico when I was there, and only three weeks late."

Success—and most importantly, happiness—are no longer fugitives to David Janssen.

C. W. POST—
"JUST A LITTLE BIT BETTER"

by DAVE HILL

The February wind was bitter that day in 1891 when the forty-year-old bankrupt stood on the steps of the Battle Creek, Michigan, City Hall, auctioning off his personal goods. Broken in health as well as wealth, he stood close to tears as he saw his most treasured gun go for a ridiculously low price. The future seemed to lay as bleak before him as the wintery sky above.

And, in 1903, the same man made a net profit of over a million dollars. Today, 60 years later, his name—well, have you ever heard of *"Postum"* or *"Post Toasties?"* C. W. Post now is recognized as one of the great business successes of the past century. This is the story of that man, the man who built his future by making things "just a little bit better."

When he auctioned off his goods that day in 1891, Post was paying off a string of debts incurred while living at the famous Battle Creek Sanitarium. He and his wife had come there from Texas a short time before, destitute after failure of his health and his milling business in Texas. At the sanitarium he met Dr. W. K. Kellogg who said later that he found Post "in a wheelchair, greatly emaciated . . . and he paid his bills with blankets salvaged from his Texas mill . . ."

At the sanitarium Post developed an interest in health foods and their health-restoring powers. He became a man obsessed. But, obsession or no, he was soon on his feet again and he gave health foods all the credit. They had done wonders for him—why not for others? Where a lesser man would have simply rejoiced in his own recovery, Post saw a great frontier of opportunity beckoning. He saw that this was something for the millions.

Soon Post had his own sanitarium, using his recently developed theories of health foods—the La Vita Inn. Before long, Battle Creek became known as "Foodtown, U.S.A."

Not satisfied with small success, Post traveled to France to study under the famous French physician, Jean Charcot. One of his fellow pupils, it might be noted was a man named Sigmund Freud. Next Post went to Bavaria and studied with Father Sebastian Kneip, famed for his "back-to-nature" cures.

Coming home, Post was full of ideas—but the biggest was strictly his own. Coffee he could not stand, both on dietary grounds and because it was "narcotic." Remembering hard times in Texas, he made some "Texas coffee"—roasted chicory and wheat. Other men would have let it go at that—he had developed a beverage which suited his needs—but not Post. He saw a product that could be sold.

For two years he studied and experimented, finally developing a drink he called "instant Postum." Investing a whopping $68.76, he set up a shop behind his little La Vita Inn in January, 1895.

Soon he had packages of Postum ready to sell. All he needed now, it seemed, was a market. Taking an armful, he called on a little store in Battle Creek. "Nothing doing," he was told. Undaunted, he went to Grand Rapids and walked into the biggest grocery store in town.

"It's absolutely useless to sell that," the grocer said. "Look." He pointed to a stack of balelike packages of something called Caramel Coffee he'd bought from the Battle Creek Sanitarium years before. "Some years I sell one package, some years none. There is no demand. You'd better go and get into a business where there is a market."

"There will be a demand, soon enough," Post said, walking out.

He went straight to the office of the Grand Rapids newspaper and entered an ad. Soon his advertising had created a demand—and business boomed. Quickly and with the insight of genius, Post realized the enormity of his discovery.

Advertising, as a selling tool, was still a virgin science. Many companies refused to "stoop" to it. Most advertising, in the early

1900s, was for patent medicines. Often a firm would find bankers withdrawing credit when they began to advertise.

This didn't stop Post—instead, it inspired him. He began to advertise, creating single-handedly almost every device practiced by Madison Avenue today. Alexander Woollcott, in a moment of humorous insight, called Post the "Henry Ford of the digestive tract."

Before long, his company showed a profit of $260,000—a far cry from his meager beginnings.

"What are you going to do with the profits?" asked an associate.

"I'm going to stick it all right back into advertising," said Post.

"It's not enough to sell food. After you get it halfway down the customer's throat with advertising, you've got to make them swallow it."

This, too, was a pioneering venture—and it reaped rich rewards. Before long, other Post products appeared—Post Toasties for one. This had originally come out under the odd name of "Elijah's Manna." Some religious groups had taken offense, and he'd changed to the name we know it under today.

Besides pioneering in advertising, Post was ahead of his time in his health-diet theories. Scientists today, with much deeper knowledge of the subjects, admit to the rightness of many of his claims. When Post claimed, "There's a reason," as he did on his early advertisements for Grape Nuts, he was stating a simple scientific truth.

On the road to the factories in Battle Creek, Post placed a sign reading "The Road to Wellville." He should have added—"and to success." For to C. W. Post, the road back to health was also the road to success.

DR. SCHOLL—
FOOTSTEPS TO SUCCESS

by BOB FERGUSON

A woman shopper strolled slowly down Chicago's Wabash Avenue, burdened by a stack of packages and supported by a pair of aching, burning feet.

Suddenly she was confronted by a tall, well-dressed gentleman with a smiling face and the erect carriage of a drum major. Sympathetically inquiring if her feet were troubling her, he suggested he might be able to help, steered her into a nearby shop and invited her to sit down. He then pulled up a shoe-fitter's stool, removed her high-heeled shoes and inspected them and her feet. After disappearing into a back room, he returned with a shoe box and fitted the woman to a handsome pair of walking shoes.

"You'll be more comfortable now," he said. "Please accept the shoes with my compliments."

Whereupon he strode out.

"Who," gasped the shopper, "was that?"

"That," said a man standing nearby, "was Dr. Scholl."

And so another person became aware that the name which has become synonymous with "foot comfort" actually belongs to a living, breathing human being.

The possessor of one of the most widely known and readily recognized names in the world is William M. Scholl, M.D., who for the past half century has been tirelessly carrying out a crusade to bring relief to aching feet.

Testifying to his success are ten manufacturing plants in the United States and six foreign countries and 424 "Dr. Scholl's

Foot Comfort Shops," scattered through 57 nations. In addition to these directly controlled product outlets, Dr. Scholl's foot aids and remedies are sold in thousands of shoe, drug, department and variety stores all over the world.

Dr. Scholl's story is the story of a man with an idea, ambition and perseverance.

The doctor himself does not consider his accomplishments unusual; he feels that all of us have the potential to become whatever we want to be.

"If you believe in yourself, believe in your ideas and are willing to work for them," says the doctor, "you can make your dreams come true."

His formula for success might be summed up as, "When you get an idea, don't think it out—work it out." The personal story of Dr. Scholl is dramatic proof that his advice works.

One of a family of thirteen children, young William Scholl discovered early that the routine of life on a dairy farm near La Porte, Indiana, was little to his liking. His interests lay along other lines. When he was fifteen he showed an aptitude for working with leather by designing and sewing a complete set of harness. This entailed building the tools with which he worked, making his own waxed thread, cutting the straps from full side leather, and putting it all together with 132,000 hand-sewn stitches. The "jig"—a device for holding the leather while he worked on it—may be seen today in the exhibit room of his main plant in Chicago.

From this beginning in leathercraft, Billy Scholl "picked up" shoe work and soon found himself serving as unofficial cobbler to his family. To expand his knowledge and to put his newfound talent on a paying basis, he became apprenticed to a La Porte shoemaker.

However, this didn't satisfy him for long. He soon mastered the cobbler's trade and, in a move that was to prove prophetic of the man, sought wider horizons. He moved to Chicago and a job in a shoe store where he proved a fine craftsman, and also made the discovery that he had a flair for selling.

Dr. Scholl believes that it was the early Chicago experiences which showed him the course his life was to take. His work in the shoe store led the young man to two conclusions: feet were horribly abused by their owners, and nothing much was being done about it. Also, somewhere in his life, he had learned that conditions remain unchanged only as long as nobody changes them.

This, then, was the crossroads for young Mr. Scholl. He had a choice of remaining what he was, a skilled craftsman and talented salesman, or embarking on a new career. He chose the latter.

Because he knew that people the world over were plagued with aching feet, because he believed this did not have to be and because he had faith in his own ability, he set forth on a self-appointed mission to become foot doctor to the world. He had found a goal. Now he planned his method of reaching it, and set to work.

But young Billy Scholl was faced with two problems. He had a job but no savings and, aside from his own untrained observations, knew nothing about human feet. But this didn't stop him or even slow him down.

He arranged to work at night so that he could attend medical school during the day. He supplemented his regular curriculum at Illinois Medical College and Chicago Medical College by studying every bit of literature then in existence which had anything to do with feet.

By the time he graduated with his M.D. in 1904, he had designed and patented his first arch support. So efficient was it that "Dr. Scholl's Foot-Eazer" still is one of the largest-selling items in the company's line of more than a thousand different products. It differs from the 1904 model only in refinement of design.

Now that he had his beginning, the young physician and inventor turned his talents to manufacturing and merchandising. His first "factory" was a store-front cubbyhole at 285 West Madison Street in Chicago where he and another young man turned out arch supports for sale to customers who came in for personal fittings.

He soon discovered such an operation had its limitations. So again seeking wider horizons, Dr. Scholl packed up a supply of Foot-Eazers and walked from shoe store to shoe store selling them—expanding his retail outlets.

But then, with about two thousand arch supports on the market, the infant industry suffered what was a near-fatal blow. The Foot-Eazers started coming back. Made of leather and Swedish steel, they proved vulnerable to perspiration and soon rusted.

"It was discouraging, all right," remembers Dr. Scholl. "Here I was, just getting a good start and it looked as though my business career already had ended."

However, instead of giving up, declaring bankruptcy or simply refunding his customers' money, the doctor went to work and revamped his arch support, substituting rustproof German silver for steel. He then replaced, at no additional cost, every Foot-Eazer he had sold.

"Actually, I gained from the experience," he says today. "By standing behind my product to such an extent, I proved my good faith and was rewarded with the trust and respect of all my customers. I also proved to myself that no obstacles, no matter how difficult, are insurmountable."

This refusal to bow to adversity may be found in all successful men. Every situation has its pitfalls, its setbacks. Things hardly ever come out exactly right the first time they are tried. When you put an idea to work, you must stick with it. And when a bad situation arises, you must learn to accept it, live with it and overcome it. Nothing can be solved by trying to run away and hide.

Over this first stumbling block turned stepping-stone, Dr. Scholl moved forward. By 1907 his enterprise had been incorporated and moved to a new location. Through persistence and hard work he continued to widen his horizons, and his products now were being distributed across the country.

Also, many new Dr. Scholl's products now were being made and sold, and their number was increasing by leaps and bounds. Every time he got a new idea for something he thought might help to relieve an aching foot, Dr. Scholl sat down with it and worked it out. And he is still doing it. This means the line is constantly expanding because never in the company's fifty-year history has a product had to be discontinued.

His newest product, the "Ball-O-Foot Cushion"—a device made of foam rubber which protects the ball of the foot from shock and pressure—was created in the middle of the night in a hotel room in California.

"You can't always pick your spots," says Dr. Scholl. "You must go to work on an idea as soon as it strikes you. If you wait for the ideal time and place to work on it, you probably never will."

Even the United States soon proved too small for Dr. Scholl. In 1908, he jumped the border and opened a branch factory in London and sales agencies all across the continent. Today his enterprise stretches around the world.

"I don't feel a person should restrict himself," says Dr. Scholl. "No job is really too big to tackle. I've always felt that if I've come this far, there's no reason why I shouldn't go a little farther."

Dr. Scholl has come a long way from the Indiana farm boy who went to work and made a set of harness. But, unfolded step by step, his story contains no miracles or mysteries unknown to the rest of us. It is simply the putting to work of ideas.

"Whenever I get an idea, I try it out," says Dr. Scholl. "I would rather know for certain that it is no good than do nothing about it and wonder if it is good."

This is the secret of Dr. Scholl. No secret at all, really. It is the practice of following thought with action, a tried and true formula for success that has been proved many times and will be proved again.

Perhaps it's your turn.

DR. JAMES TURPIN—HIS SUCCESS HAS NO PRICE TAG

by ELEANORE PAGE HAMILTON

The infamous Walled City of Kowloon lies in a ten-square-block area of decay within the modern Chinese metropolis of that name. Across the seething harbor, the skyline of Hong Kong's capital shines in splendid kinship with progressive cities everywhere. Tourists who come to these British colonies savor the Oriental atmosphere and join a cosmopolitan way of life without ever becoming involved with the turbulence of people around them. It is only in the refuse-strewn alleys, on the hillsides and rooftops, and among the junks of the crowded Yaumati typhoon shelter that one comes face-to-face with the realities of incredible human suffering.

This is the setting for which Dr. James Turpin traded a $60,000-a-year medical practice in Coronado, California. "These people need me," he explains simply. "Tens of thousands of desperate refugees from communism have converged on Hong Kong, swelling the already overpopulated sectors of the poor. And because I am selfish, I need them too. I like the inner feeling of satisfaction I get from helping them."

It was in September of 1962, while Typhoon Wanda raged, that "Dr. Jim" arrived in Hong Kong with his wife Martha, four children and a cortege of volunteers. There was something prophetic about that storm. The efforts of this initial group spread over the island and adjoining Kowloon with a like vigor. In less than three years, a saying of the villagers of Lyemun in Hong Kong had been brought to life by the organization called *Project Concern:* "Under Heaven—one family."

Through the generosity of a Chinese doctor, a spacious house was placed at their disposal. A houseboat clinic was being remodeled for their use from a 65-foot cargo junk. But Dr. Jim did not wait for its completion to plunge into the problems of the hurt humanity he had come so many miles to help.

The Walled City, never a place of easy access, was his first target. The only way in is on foot; and there is seldom a way out. Some twenty-five thousand wretched souls inhabit this section of Kowloon that Dr. Jim says has been aptly named "Hell on Earth." Here, disease flourishes on poverty and an appalling lack of water and sewage facilities. Babies are born by the hundreds into this fetid environment every year.

"This impact of poverty is not inheritable." Dr. Jim maintains. "The idea that the Chinese exist contentedly on a handful of rice is a fallacy. They don't like it any more than we would."

Before he came to Kowloon, some British nurses had tried to do something about this sector. They had gained permission to operate a Child Care Center there. It was desperately inadequate. Hence, the Doctor's offer to work with them in the forbidden area was God-sent. "Abandon all hope, O ye who enter here," he thought as he picked his way along the narrow, dirty passageways that served as streets. "Well, mankind was not meant to live without hope. We'll get to know these people intimately and start a program of self-help to teach them how to survive."

Almost immediately, he noticed a small, sloe-eyed boy waiting patiently in line for his daily milk ration. An open sore purpled his ankle. Leaning down for a better look, Dr. Jim discovered a piece of broken chain imbedded in the inflamed flesh. An interpreter revealed that the child had been pinioned to an old cot while his parents worked as laborers. He had simply pulled himself free like a dog from a steel trap.

Actually, this child was well-off by local standards. Thousands of Hong Kong urchins have no fixed abode. They live in the hills or among the 135,000 pavement dwellers in the city, with no known human ties—unless they are adopted by a criminal gang.

It wasn't long before Dr. Jim's tall figure and silvering crew cut were a familiar sight in the Walled City. He became a personal Pied Piper to the children who followed him everywhere he went in the gloomy corridors. Now they are lined up early each morning, hours before *Project Concern* opens its clinic. There, they will be given the only nourishment they may get all day—milk, a chewable vitamin tablet and a high-protein wafer.

When the houseboat was finished, it was christened *Yauh Oi* (Brotherly Love). Dr. Jim established his family "in residence" below decks. Above are the registration desk, examination rooms, pharmacy and laboratories of the floating clinic. A smaller converted hull, the *Ming Ling*, is anchored alongside to provide X-ray, dental and eye-ear-nose-and-throat facilities.

The milk-and-vitamin routine here is called a "survival party." Dr. Jim says it is easier to prevent diseases this way than to cure them. Besides, eager hands reaching from the junks and sampans that bob endlessly on the watery terrain give confidence to the more fearful boat people. There are some 50,000 of them in the Yaumati shelter. "These Tanka folk have a saying— 'water bred, water dead'—and will live and die afloat," said Dr. Jim. "We had to bring our clinic to them because they are too superstitious to go ashore."

Sampans nudging the clinic boats is a continuous sound now. Often a more cumbersome junk ties up to the *Yauh Oi* for the duration of an illness. And the Tanka people come in an endless, frightened procession. They come in awe and anxiety with such maladies as tuberculosis, cholera, malaria and leprosy. Skin diseases and dysentery—*always* dysentery—plague them.

"We go wherever the need is greatest," is the way Dr. Jim describes the widening circle of activity for *Project Concern*. Word came to us that there were about 12,500 near-destitute villagers in a squatter area—the Jordan Valley Resite. Our medical teams set up a clinic there in an old abandoned cemetery office."

Coming along the docks to the *Yauh Oi* one morning, a medical team was attracted by a dense crowd in the duck market. Pushing into the center of the noisy throng, they saw a man seated on the ground with an infant in each arm. A sign with scrawled Chinese letters proclaimed: "Babies for Sale." Dr. Jim commented that the now-and-then sale or even the destruction of a female baby was not prompted by a lack of affection. It was always due to the survival factor.

The Orient is a crossroads of new ideas and ancient philosophies. It isn't always easy to combat needle magic or bizarre potions. Showing them love and concern through personal contact is Dr. Jim's way. He feels that there is a world-wide eagerness to learn today. Many who work with him are Chinese. And they have found the poor with their problems of overpopulation anxious to better their own lot through such teachings as planned parenthood. It is easier for them to learn from their own people, within the concept of their own traditions.

Since 1963, the addition of Dr. Jack Wong to the staff made it possible to create two medical teams to serve three clinics—each with a registered doctor, several Chinese unregistered physicians, a lab technician, a registrar and a nurse. Volunteers man the feeding programs.

With everything going well in Hong Kong, the time had come for Dr. James Turpin to move on. He had longed planned an operation in Vietnam. In the village of Dampao, two hundred miles northeast of Saigon, he set up a clinic in a thatched hut with bamboo walls. The word went out that the American doctor had come to help the Vietnamese and any of the primitive mountain people who would come to him!

Surprisingly, the Montagnards poured from the Koho Mountains where one hundred thousand of them lived in animallike deprivation. Their undernourished bodies were wracked by the same diseases that harassed the Chinese in Hong Kong and Kowloon. Worse still, many were fear-ridden by godless philosophies and acts that they were ill equipped to understand.

It was in this unlikely tropical place that a sort of miracle began to take shape. Young men of Montagnard stock asked questions. They were joined by Vietnamese who came to watch the doctor at work. "Why *here* is the hope of these people," he realized. "I can teach *them* to care for their own kind."

With the co-operation of the South Vietnamese government, Dr. Jim organized the young men and women of the area into a corps of aides. When he returned to the United States recently, he left behind a hospital that treats 600 a day, as well as 35 capable Village Medical Officers who can administer 13 basic drugs for 90 percent of the common diseases. Many will go into 25 villages in the vicinity to teach health and sanitation.

What is the future of *Project Concern?* Dr. Jim believes it is unlimited. When he has completed his current lecture and fund-raising tour, he will go back to Asia to continue his work, leaving "Postmaster, San Diego, California" as his mailing address. His blue-grey eyes are clear and full of faith as he assures his listeners that "We have not seen any combination of privations which defy our ability to correct in the three years we have been in existence."

ART WALTON—PERSISTENCY, PRESCRIPTION FOR SUCCESS

by ELIZABETH LELLO

"Write a story about my success? You're putting me on!" The vibrant voice came ringing over the telephone, followed by a boyish laugh. "I don't think of myself as outstanding."

"Anybody who can buy a broken-down drug store and turn it into a booming business in eight years is outstanding. How old are you?"

The reply was almost apologetic.

"Thirty-two."

That seemed awfully young from where I stood. I wanted to meet this Art Walton and find out how he had done it. We made a date for the next day and met in his office.

"Art," I asked, picking up the threads of our telephone conversation, "have you always wanted to be a pharmacist?"

He laughed. "No, but when I was going to high school in Los Angeles, a neighbor said I looked like a pharmacist. I still don't know how a pharmacist is supposed to look but her remark sent me down to the corner drug store to talk to Max Loman, the owner. What a guy! He became a second father to me.

"I started taking Latin and Chemistry and other subjects I'd need in pharmacy and I began to concentrate on grades. I had been sliding by on C's but after I had a goal I got A's and B's. When things got tough I'd go down and talk to Mr. Loman. I still do."

"Did anyone else help you?"

"My wife LaVonne. We met when we were juniors in high school and married right after graduation. She liked the idea of my becoming a pharmacist so we went up north to the University of California. Talk about togetherness. She worked days in a bank and I was on the swing shift at a rubber company nights. We only saw each other on weekend!"

"When did you study?"

"Whenever I got a chance. My grades were okay, except for ROTC. I got a D in that, which temporarily washed me up, although I could have gone to summer school and made it up. Instead, we wrote to schools all over the country inquiring about their courses. The University of Colorado was the only one that seemed enthusiastic about having me."

I smiled.

"It's true. They wrote a really friendly letter and said we could borrow on the University Fund for tuition and books, so that's where we went.

"We had $25.00 and a model T to travel in. Oh, and LaVonne was pregnant."

I shuddered.

"It wasn't bad. We slept in the car and ate as little as possible. We didn't have sense enough to worry. Anyway, worry only stops you from getting where you want to go. We enjoyed the trip!"

"Then came the trailer! Did you ever live in a tent through a Colorado winter? The trailer we lived in was the nearest thing to it. No piped-in water. There was a bucket under the sink and if we forgot to empty it, and we forgot all of the time, it overflowed and LaVonne had to mop the floor. When the bed pulled down we had to call signals to pass each other! You had to keep pumping the stove if you wanted it to cook, and the kerosene heater kept the ceiling hot and the floor icy.

"When LaVonne was about five months along, she tripped over that darned bed and fell against the corner of a low cupboard. She was crying and moaning and I thought for sure the baby was going to come, but he didn't, not that boy! Artie waited his full time and kept his mother in labor for 36 hours. Weighed over eight pounds.

"Anyway, when she fell, I thought, this is for the birds! I'm going to get a job and take care of my wife and to heck with being a pharmacist! I told LaVonne, but she kept crying and saying, 'No, no, no. You're going to finish college!' So to hush her up I agreed. Then the doctor said she would be okay so we went on working and studying and getting ready for the baby."

"LaVonne had a job?"

"Yes, in the library, and I worked in Vetsville on the trash truck and on the roads."

"So you stuck to it and graduated, then came back to Los Angeles. Did you go right to work as a druggist?"

He shook his head.

"It wasn't that easy. They raised the requirements before I could take the Board examination. I had to have a fifth year!

"We used to kid about how they were going to repossess the baby because he wasn't paid for and we had to start reducing our loan from the University, so I got a job as an apprentice pharmacist at a store in Torrance and went to night school at Southern Cal. I made $65.00 a week. It just wasn't enough and I asked for a raise. The boss said 'No,' so I quit."

Art's jaw set as he remembered, his eyes seeing back to that time.

"Well, I finished my shift and went home full of anger, expecting to explode to LaVonne. She met me at the door, crying. They had turned off our water, light and gas!

"We looked at each other in silence for a moment and knew we would have to do something we had so far avoided—go to a relative for help. LaVonne's uncle loaned us some money and pulled us out of the hole.

"I got another job and continued night school. My new job paid $75.00 a week and after I finished school and passed the Board exams it went up to $125.00. Still it wasn't enough. I was working from 1:00 P.M. to 10:00 P.M. and we were just barely making ends meet, so I quit and went to work for Ciba Pharmaceutical Products as a detail man on salary plus commission."

"How old were you then?"

"Just twenty-two, but that job helped me to grow up. I couldn't get mad at the doctors if I wanted them to buy my products, so I learned to control myself.

"I kept trying to think of ways to increase my sales, and one day I remembered how they show popcorn falling all over the screen just before intermission at the movies to make people want to buy. Subliminal selling, it's called.

"Soon after that, during an interview with a doctor, I said, 'You know how it is when you sit down in a barber chair after a hard day's work. Your neck muscles are full of aching knots and your body is tense. The barber begins to massage your neck and a wonderful relaxation steals over you. That's the way our tranquilizers make you feel.' He said he'd try them!"

"With that technique my sales began to increase. I read all I could on the power of suggestion and used what I learned. In a nationwide contest I placed third and won a lot of prizes.

"Then we began to save, a little at a time, till we had $500. It seemed like a fortune.

"I like people, all kinds of people, and the Toastmaster's Club offered me an opportunity to make new friends, so I joined. One of the members was a contractor who built tract houses. He asked me if I'd like to invest some money in his project. We had that $500 lying in the bank. We hated to risk it, but I figure you've got to take a chance now and then, so I gave it to him.

"He sold that batch of houses and gave me $1,000. Doubled our money! We put the thousand into his next project and got back $2,000.

"I was ready to give up the drug business entirely and go into contracting, but one noon at 'Toastmasters' the speaker emphasized the importance of doing the thing you know best.

"What did I know best? The drug business. What had I been working toward all these years? To own my own store.

"That did it. I started looking and asking around and I found this place."

"No regrets?" I asked.

"The contractor went broke on his next development. I got out just in time!

"I wanted this store the way a kid wants Christmas! But the owner didn't want to sell to me! To him I was a poor risk, a twenty-four-year-old unknown quantity. I had to do some real subliminal selling then! I kept painting a picture of how I would display products and carry new lines, etc. Finally he was convinced that I really knew the drug business and we came to terms. We put in our $2,000 plus $3,000 borrowed from a relative, and the store was ours."

"And now you're the prosperous owner of one of the best drug stores in San Pedro," I said.

"Two," said Art. "I'm building my second store on the other side of town."

He tried to sound modest but pride colored his voice.

The door opened and a slender ash blonde with enormous brown eyes stood in the doorway.

"Oh, excuse me!" She started to back out.

"Just a minute, honey," Art turned to me. "This is LaVonne. You really ought to be interviewing her!"

I shook hands with the pretty girl I felt I knew so well and complimented her on the success she and Art had achieved.

"You have to know what you want and then stick to it, no matter what," said LaVonne. "Abby said it in her column this morning. You've *gotta wanta!* You've gotta wanta so passionately that nothing and no one can discourage you!"

"That about sums it up," said Art.

LINCOLN'S KEY TO SUCCESS

My dear Sir:

I have just reached home and found your letter. If you are resolutely determined to make a lawyer of yourself, the thing is more than half done already. It is but a small matter whether you read *with* anybody or not. I did not read with anyone. Get the books and read and study them till you understand them in their principal features, and that is the main thing. It is of no consequence to be in a large town while you are reading. I read at New Salem, which never had three hundred people living in it. The *books,* and your *capacity* for understanding them, are just the same in all places.

Always bear in mind that your own resolution to succeed is more important than any other one thing.

A. Lincoln

The above letter was written to Isham Reavis, a young lad who asked Abraham Lincoln for advice. It was written while the Great Emancipator was in Springfield, Illinois, and before he was elected the sixteenth President of the United States. Lincoln called his letter "Advice to a young boy who aspires to become a lawyer." If you have read the letter and did not catch what he terms the most important attribute to becoming a success, then read it through again.

Lincoln did not believe a man must go to a large or even a small city to become successful. He pointed out that he began his climb to success in a little town which never had more than three hundred people living in it.

But of greater importance is Lincoln's key to success: In the last paragraph of the letter, he admonishes the young boy to always bear in mind that "your own resolution to succeed is more important than any other one thing."

For additional information about Napoleon Hill products please contact the following locations:

Napoleon Hill World Learning Center
Purdue University Calumet
2300 173rd Street
Hammond, IN 46323-2094

Judith Williamson, Director
Uriel "Chino" Martinez, Assistant/Graphic Designer

Telephone: 219-989-3173 or 219-989-3166
email: nhf@calumet.purdue.edu

Napoleon Hill Foundation
University of Virginia-Wise
College Relations Apt. C
1 College Avenue
Wise, VA 24293

Don Green, Executive Director
Annedia Sturgill, Executive Assistant

Telephone: 276-328-6700
email: napoleonhill@uvawise.edu

Website: www.naphill.org